The Joseph Rowntree Foundation

The Joseph Rowntree Foundation has supported this project as part of its programme of research and innovative development projects, which it hopes will be of value to policy makers, practitioners and service users. The facts presented and views expressed in this report are, however, those of the authors and not necessarily those of the Foundation

—— SUPPORTED BY ——

About Demos

Who we are
Demos is the think tank everyone should be able to lives that contribute to democratic idea into pr ways that make them more effective and legitimate.

What we work on
We focus on six areas: public services; science and technology; cities and public space; people and communities; arts and culture; and global security.

Who we work with
Our partners include policy-makers, companies, public service providers and social entrepreneurs. Demos is not linked to any party but we work with politicians across political divides. Our international network – which extends across Eastern Europe, Scandinavia, Australia, Brazil, India and China – provides a global perspective and enables us to work across borders.

How we work
Demos knows the importance of learning from experience. We test and improve our ideas in practice by working with people who can make change happen. Our collaborative approach means that our partners share in the creation and ownership of new ideas.

What we offer
We analyse social and political change, which we connect to innovation and learning in organisations. We help our partners show thought leadership and respond to emerging policy challenges.

How we communicate
As an independent voice, we can create debates that lead to real change. We use the media, public events, workshops and publications to communicate our ideas. All our books can be downloaded free from the Demos website.

www.demos.co.uk

ISBN 1 84180 149 6
Copy edited by Julie Pickard
Designed and typeset
by Divamedia, Bristol
Printed in the United Kingdom
by Lookers, Poole
All photography from Cardiff, Preston &
Swindon © Paul Box 2005

For further information and subscription
details please contact:
Demos
Third Floor
Magdalen House
136 Tooley Street
London SE1 2TU
Telephone: 0207 367 4200
email: mail@demos.co.uk
web: www.demos.co.uk

DEMOS

Building
everyday
democracy

People Make Places:

growing the public life of cities

Melissa Mean

Charlie Tims

DEM◐S

contents

People Make Places: growing the public life of cities

Acknowledgements

We are grateful to the Joseph Rowntree Foundation for supporting this work. In particular we would like to thank Katharine Knox for her enthusiasm and encouragement throughout the project.

Many individuals at Demos helped make this project possible. We are indebted to those who were part of the team in the field: Gillian Thomas, Lilli Geissendorfer and Astrid Winkler. Gillian was also invaluable in helping to develop the research methodology. We are grateful to Tom Bentley and Catherine Fieschi for their comments and guidance; Lauren Traczykowski and Danae Bougas for their help with the background research; and Sam Hinton–Smith and Eddie Gibb for their media work.

We would like to thank our advisory group for their wise words and rapid reading of drafts – Ash Amin, Chris Brown, Alain Chiaradia, Rachel Eaton, Imtiaz Farookhi, Paul Hildreth and Marcia Lewison. A special thanks goes to Alain Chiaradia and Esenghiul Abdul-Gemil who, with the aid of Simon Lannon at Cardiff University, gave added depth to the analysis.

A big thank you to Paul Box for taking fantastic photographs. And to Andy Barnes and his team at Divamedia for designing a great looking book.

Finally, we would like to thank the people we met in Cardiff, Preston and Swindon for making this such an enjoyable project.

As ever, all errors or omissions remain our own.

Melissa Mean

Charlie Tims

July 2005

A note on the methodology.

The field research for this project was undertaken in Cardiff, Preston and Swindon over the course of a year. The research involved a good deal of what Demos calls 'deep hanging out' – spending time in the cities[1] and public spaces, observing how they worked at different times of the day and talking with a wide range of people as they went about their daily activities.

This included:

- stakeholder interviews with 15–20 stakeholders from civic, public and private sector organisations in each city
- nearly 700 interviews with members of the public in a range of public spaces in the three cities
- nine focus groups, three in each city, with the following groups: people over 65, gay people between the ages of 18 and 40, and people from black and minority ethnic (BME) groups aged between 18 and 30
- in-depth studies of over 30 public spaces in the three cities.

01.Introduction

How good a city is at facilitating exchange
determines its health – economic, social,
cultural and environmental. Public space
forms a vital conduit in this exchange process,
providing platforms for everyday interaction
and information flows – the basis and content
for the public life of cities. . .

Cities

Cities were invented to facilitate exchange – the exchange of ideas, friendships, material goods and skills. How good a city is at facilitating exchange determines its health – economic, social, cultural and environmental. Public space forms a vital conduit in this exchange process, providing platforms for everyday interaction and information flows – the basis and content for the public life of cities. At their best, public spaces act like a self-organising public service; just as hospitals and schools provide a shared resource to improve people's quality of life, public spaces form a shared spatial resource from which experiences and value are created in ways that are not possible in our private lives alone.

From the Athenian agora to the Victorian promenades and the modernist shopping precincts of the postwar town planners, specific periods of enthusiasm for public space have produced the spatial infrastructure that continues to shape the public life of our towns and cities today. This set of inherited public spaces is currently in the throws of being part supplemented, part substituted by a new wave of enthusiastic investment for public space under the tag line of urban renaissance. Regenerated quaysides, iconic architectural set pieces, cultural quarters and redesigned high streets are becoming standard kit in a growing number of our towns and cities. The government's neighbourhood renewal initiative, hospital, school and major house building programmes all promise to remake our urban environment still further.

In the midst of this building and rebuilding a degree of uncertainty is discernible. While we used to be fairly confident about where to find the public life of our towns and cities – in our parks, streets and squares – now it seems we are not so sure. The rise of privately owned corporate malls, out-of-town shopping centres and the virtual landscapes of the internet have cast doubt on the publicness of our towns and cities. Privatised space is seen to be in the ascendancy and, it is argued, this is squeezing out the possibility of shared social spaces in our cities, replacing them with a 'shopping mall culture'[2] of sanitised, frictionless consumer environments where architecture and technology are used to filter out undesirable people and groups. So far it is unclear whether the new set of public spaces created through the urban renaissance are countering this trend and proving effective hosts for shared public life and exchange between people, or whether they are adding to the loss of publicness by imitating the character of private space. Many of the shiny new quaysides and squares seem either curiously empty of people or curiously monocultural in the type of people they attract.

The mission of Demos over the past 12 months has been to take on this uncertainty and track down the public life of cities – to identify the shared spaces of interaction and exchange, the value that such spaces generate and how that value is created. We explored in depth three cities in the UK – Cardiff, Preston and Swindon – to discover and illuminate the processes by which the public life of cities more widely might be reinvigorated.

We began with the conventional public geography of parks, squares and streets to see how well they were performing as shared spaces of exchange. Then, having discovered that people were not always where they were expected to be, we opened up the search to seek out and explore other everyday spaces and places that people use and value. Our search took us to some unexpected places, sometimes challenging our preconceptions about where and what a public

space should be – from allotments and art centres to supermarket cafés and car boot sales.

What our search highlighted was the importance of understanding public space from the perspective of the participant. A new town square could be carefully, beautifully designed, but there was no guarantee that people would come and use it. People have a wide variety of motivations, needs and resources that shape their personal capacity and desire to use the communal spaces within their town or city. This sometimes creates sharp inequalities between different people's ability to participate in the wider public life of a city outside home and work.

We also found that public space is better understood less as a predetermined physical space, and more as an experience created by an interaction between people and a place. In other words, public space is co-produced through the active involvement of the user. This shift from a place-based to a user-led understanding enables the quality of public space within a neighbourhood or even a whole city to be assessed in terms of how well it supports a range of 'public experiences', such as belonging and companionship, risk-taking and adventure, and reflection and learning. In terms of current policy and practice, we found that the current safety-focused approach to public space may be hindering the development of spaces that can play host to this wider spectrum of experiences and value.

The story of this pamphlet is not one of doom and gloom, of the death and disappearance of public space. Instead, it is a story of surprises and hope, and the beginning of an expanded universe of public space. We interviewed and observed people creating shared spaces and experiences in the **most** unexpected and improbable places, cutting **across** public, commercial and community realms. **In this**

process they revealed how even commercial spaces such as supermarkets and malls could be co-opted for public ends. The implication is that there is a far wider set of opportunities and resources to influence public space for the better, but these forms of influence need to be much more sophisticated than those currently employed by policy-makers and city planners.

Individual public spaces are important in their own right. A neighbourhood park can host many special occasions, from a quiet walk for new lovers, to a mass celebration at a summer festival. But understanding what brings a public space to life also holds the potential for wider democratic learning, in particular for how other institutions and services in our cities need to work if they are to engage and generate value for people. Equally, if cities can get the micro public spaces of street corners, cafés, malls and parks to flourish in a way that simultaneously meets people's personal needs and the wider common good, then this intelligence and the patterns of interaction stimulated might just 'trickle up' and start creating patterns and value on the next scale up. From shared public spaces grow shared neighbourhoods and shared cities, and maybe beyond.

02.The promise and reality of public space

At one pole, the core ideal of public space – free and open access for all – is being undermined by a focus first and last on safety, which is creating bland, lowest-common-denominator spaces with no real power to draw or retain people. At the other, increasing diversity of lifestyles and culture is splintering public space into a patchwork of specialised monocultural enclaves. . .

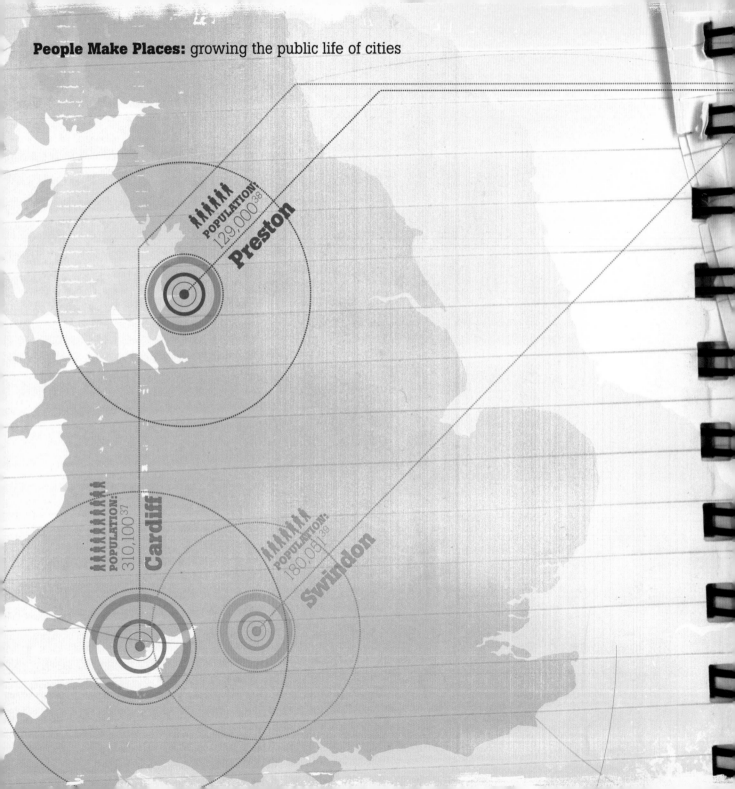

POPULATION: 129,000 [38]
Preston

POPULATION: 310,100 [37]
Cardiff

POPULATION: 180,051 [39]
Swindon

	Cardiff	Preston	Swindon
Peer places[36]	Glasgow, Newcastle and Birmingham	Newport, Stirling	Peterborough, Milton Keynes
Aspiration places	Barcelona, Baltimore	Manchester, Liverpool and Leeds	Ipswich, Halifax (Canada) and Bristol
CPA rating	Fair (proxy rating)[40]	Good[41]	Weak[42]
Non-white-British population[43]	8.4%	16.8%	4.8%
Commuters in/out Per day	69,800 in; 23,100 out[44]	20,000 in; 22,000 out[45]	46,088 in; out (n/a)[46]
University population	22,000[47]	32,610[48]	0
Pink economy[49] (people per gay facility)	4078	4321	9476
% of under 16-year-olds	20.6%[50]	21%[51]	21%[52]
% of over 75-year-olds	7.2%[53]	7%[54]	6.2%[55]
Indices of Deprivation Rank	18 (out of 22)[56]	59[57]	171[58]
Unemployment rate[59]	4.5%	3.4%	2.5%
Average house price[60]	£158,177	£65,881	£153,887 (plus 6.8% in last year)
Average gross weekly earnings	£448.30	£426.21	£574.50

CPA, comprehensive performance assessment

Cities

are like complex organisms.[3] Their characters emerge from millions of daily interactions between soft and hard factors: employment patterns, the demographic profile of the population, the presence or absence of a university, the quality of public transport, the range of cultural and civic organisations, the quality of the housing stock and so on; the list is probably endless.

This creates a radical variation in the public character of towns and cities and shapes a corresponding variation in quality of life at both the individual and collective level within each place. It is vital therefore to be able to unpick and understand how these constituent place-based character traits interact and how they might be guided to better enhance the quality of life for people in them.

Public spaces offer a tangible and everyday arena in which these soft and hard factors intersect and come together. It is within the physical spaces of our towns and cities that people encounter one another on a daily basis and share experiences with people beyond their immediate circle of friends, family and work colleagues. It is where people are obliged to relate to others' behaviour, ideas and preferences as they go about meeting their own personal needs. Parks, streets and other public spaces provide the necessary bandwidth for the flow of information between people; they are where we learn who we live with, what they look like and what they do.

This chapter introduces the three places we studied in depth for this project, and sets their public space in a wider context of ideas and public policy. Cardiff, Preston and Swindon show how influential different kinds of public space can be. While each is distinctive, each also represents a type of urban experience that it holds in common with other towns and cities. These characteristics also reflect some essential ideas about public space that have shaped our towns and cities during particular eras and with this illustrate the persistent gap between the promise of the ideal of public space and the reality of people's experience.

Cardiff: public space glamour

Over the last decade a burst of investment, energy and competition between cities has reshaped many urban centres. As a torchbearer for this urban renaissance, Cardiff has not had it so good in a long time. New employers, a booming university and cranes across the skyline form the backdrop for a bustling city. For Cardiff we could read Leeds, Newcastle or Birmingham. The city has pioneered the full-on wave of 1990s' style urban regeneration, with its strong emphasis on culture and design-led retail-friendly public space. Its former docks now boast a promenade of hotels, apartments, bars, restaurants and an opera house. This style of development is sprinkled across the city with marble squares and trendy bar quarters opening up. Chasing champion league status for shopping, the city has plans for redeveloping its shopping district still further. However, the many people who fall outside the target market of the city's redevelopment strategies are left cold by all the activity going on around them. Those who are not young and affluent feel little is relevant to them and are made to feel more invisible in the public life of the city. In particular, the Somali community of Bute Town continue to feel overlooked, with many other residents regarding the area as a kind of no-man's land sandwiched between the resurgent city centre and bay.

Preston: public space tradition

Preston is old, civic and hungry for recognition. It is bucking the trend of many northern contemporaries with its growing population, fairly mixed economic base, growing university and amicable race relations among a diverse population. Its existing infrastructure has got the city this far, but as city leaders hurry to build, expand and re-brand, they are in danger of leaving some Prestonians behind. Its public space reflects this tension. Preston is a cradle of Victorian public spaces – landscaped civic gardens and a collection of market squares in the centre, complemented by rolling parkland in the suburbs. These investments made 150 years ago have served the city well, but Preston is divided over what kinds of public spaces might serve it well for the future. Plans to redevelop the market area and demolish the iconic bus station are proving extremely controversial, while for some the desultory redevelopment of Preston Marina represents an unsettling portent of things to come.

Preston reflects the Victorian legacy of public improvement through public space. Victorian reformers saw such investment as a way to civilise and improve the conditions of the rapidly growing urban working classes.[4] Seaside piers, urban parks, promenades and city squares were the prescription. However, despite the public ideal many Victorian public parks and gardens were in fact carefully managed and controlled spaces, with the middle classes often preferring private gardens and policed shopping districts to the general throng of the city.[5] Equally, the moneyed classes tended to enjoy the new urban parks from the safety of a horse-drawn carriage, unsure whether the freshly imported presence of nature in cities had sufficiently improved the working classes to make free mixing permissible.[6]

Swindon: public space amnesia

Mention public space to anyone in Swindon and they are quick to tell you that there isn't any. In the rush to build houses for slum-cleared Londoners after the war and successive local manufacturing and service sector booms, public space somehow got forgotten. However, with the town's productivity now on the wane, its lack of cultural and social infrastructure has become a visible chip on its shoulder.

Caught in a web of motorways, roundabouts and bypasses, Swindon town centre has no obvious public spaces other than its covered shopping malls and connecting walkways that run through office blocks. Its potential squares are filled with cars while its central library has been relegated to a Portakabin. Public space is squeezed and coincidental – the forecourt of a garage, the pavement outside a kebab shop, the remnants of the Old Town, standing grandly on a hill. The result is a two-speed town. In the fast lane orbiting commuters raid Swindon by car for the monthly supermarket-shop and their 9 to 5 jobs, returning to comfortable rural villages or executive homes on the edge of town. Meanwhile, those living in the centre ponder how they can get to the nice country parks that feel just out of reach on the fringes of the town. The civic leaders of Swindon have begun to realise what the band of committed activist residents have long known – that the town's public spaces matter, and they need some attention. At the moment, it seems the council's main plan is to refit the commercially focused town centre to appeal more to the affluent village dwellers.

In its lack of a public focal point, Swindon points to a much older ideal of public space that still influences our expectations, however implicitly. With its elevated, open colonnade the Agora of ancient Athens suggested a civic culture based on openness, accountability and accessibility. It was literally a meeting place, acting as the space where politics, commerce, information and entertainment were fused together. The Agora was not only where the general assembly came together to conduct political business, it was also a market, theatre space and display place for community information.[7] Though again, reality was not so rosy as the ideal promised. As Richard Sennett reminds us, the Athenian Agora was far from being universally inclusive. Of the 320,000 inhabitants of Athens it is estimated that only 20,000–40,000 of them were deemed citizens and thus able to participate in the Agora; women, slaves, foreigners and free-labourers were all barred.[8]

Public space, public good, public policy

Supplanting the dark predictions of the previous two decades during which academics and commentators decried the decline, and even death, of public space,[9] the current wave of rebuilding and regeneration reflects a new optimism that the persistent gap between the ideal of public space and its reality can be closed. Indeed, current government policies for public space in the UK[10] are concerned with trying to use investment in places and spaces as a vehicle to counter some of the negative trends that have been undermining the efficacy of public space to contribute to social, economic and democratic goals. These negative trends include growing inequality, social fragmentation and institutional decline – all fuelled by the growth in private wealth.

The most important of these negative trends and the efforts to counter them involve moving from:

- social distrust to community efficacy
- splintering cities to social inclusion
- privatised space to quality of place.

Distrust of other people's behaviour and the search for shared efficacy

In surveys during the 1950s, more than two-thirds of British people said that most people could be trusted. When the same question was asked in the late 1990s, the 'trusters' had fallen to 29 per cent of the population.[11] Increased choice, diversity and mobility are blamed for a decline in what sociologists call 'traditional trust' – the trust that comes from our immersion in traditional communities and familiarities. This erosion of trust has become a popular refrain of politicians and the media alike in debates ranging from government policy on genetically modified food to pensions. There is no doubt that improving public space is seen as a way to increase people's trust of one another. As one recent report by CABE Space puts it, 'When properly designed and cared for, [public spaces] bring communities together, provide meeting places and foster social ties'.[12] The dominant response to the loss of trust in other people's behaviour, however, has been to get serious about safety.

The safety maxim is evident in our now security-heavy urban landscape where no town is complete without blanket CCTV coverage and a shopping mall policed by private security guards. It is evident in the increased nervousness about what kind of activity is safe in public space and the urge among public and private agencies alike to try and 'risk manage everything'[13] – down to the risk of conkers falling on a park-walker's head. It is also evident in the weight of government effort given to trying to control anti-social behaviour and in ministerial appeals for more 'respect'.

It is questionable whether the current safety maxim is making anyone more trusting of other people's behaviour or anyone more confident about their participation in public space. Psychologist Dorothy Rowe explains how, for an example, an older person living alone might call for more security measures, but this is just a more socially acceptable way of asking for attention; his or her deeper, unspoken need is for family, friends and social support.[14] This is a need that will be left untouched by the addition of another CCTV camera and therefore his or her fear of making use of public space will remain. Equally, the 'crack-down' on anti-social behaviour in town centres has become a narrowly negative model about trying to neutralise binge drinking with on-the-spot fines and 'sin-bins', rather than a positive model of trying to encourage and provide space for other types of more social behaviour.

From splintering cities to social inclusion

As consumers, we live in a world of mass customisation and specialisation. Increased choice, personal freedom and cultural diversity mean that people are increasingly keen and able to craft their own unique lifestyle and identity. This can be a liberating and empowering process for many people and it should not be discounted or condemned.[15] But the impact on public space is significant: many of our towns and cities are losing their shared spaces because, simply put, people have less in common with others to share. Dutch academic Marteen Hajer describes this process as people adopting a highly selective 'al la carte approach' to using public space.[16] Simultaneously, economic inequality between both people and places has grown steadily over the last generation, creating more extreme disparities between people sharing the same public infrastructure. The result is that not all people are served equally by the public spaces that are available to them. Increasingly, commercial operators employ a policy of target marketing and seeking out premium users, thus excluding people who are deemed lower-value users.

The policy response is to treat public space as an opportunity for developing shared, non-economic identities to offset the effects of this inequality:

> *Public spaces have a critical role in creating pride in the places where we live which, in turn is essential to building community cohesion.*
>
> Office of the Deputy Minister[17]

People Make Places: growing the public life of cities

> *By being open to all regardless of ethnic origin, age or gender, they represent a democratic forum for society.*

CABE Space[18]

Privatisation of public space and quality of place

New forms of governance are reconfiguring the collective life of our towns and cities. Conventional public spaces such as parks and squares provided and run by the state are being supplemented and in some cases squeezed out by a wider mix of spaces with different governance arrangements. These arrangements include corporate governance in shopping malls, business parks, entertainment complexes and Business Improvement Districts, but also civic governance as seen in the trend towards community ownership of assets such as community centres and parks. Many see this as the progressive privatisation of public space, reducing the pool of openly shared public spaces in towns and cities. As Toronto- and Australia-based academics Shearing and Wood describe, many of these new governance forms look very much like conventional public spaces but each carries with it a different set of expectations and obligations on those using it, often with implicit or explicit limits on who can use it and how.[19] For example, membership fees limit who can use a privately owned gym, wearing certain clothes can get you barred from a mall, or being from a particular faith background may be necessary to use a particular facility.

One policy response associated with these changes is the effort to promote public space as an economic asset worthy of private and commercial investment. This investment can reinforce private control of previously public spaces, but it can also encourage a recognition that the degree of welcome and accessibility found by diverse visitors contributes to the economic vitality of a particular place.[20]

The thrust of much government policy, in the UK and elsewhere, over the last decade, has been to find new ways of channelling private investment into public infrastructure and other public goods, partly in response to growing private wealth. The hybrid forms of governance described above reflect this 'partnership' logic, and illustrate the widely held view that investing in the public realm can generate commercial return and is an ingredient of competitiveness of towns, cities and regions.

Within this, public space is being increasingly recognised as critical to the 'quality of place package' with which towns and cities compete against one another for visitors, firms and inhabitants.[21] As a recent report from CABE Space puts it, 'Companies are attracted to locations that offer well-designed, well-managed public places and these in turn attract customers, employers and services.'[22]

The implications of this trend cut both ways. The value of public spaces and places extends to many private interests and organisations, and creates new opportunities for sharing responsibility and investment between them. However, the new rules governing such spaces may influence and control how they are used and by whom in ways that are not explained by the classical definition of free, universal open space in which strangers can interact and co-exist.

Public spaces in the balance

Are these public policies and investments working successfully? There are some positive effects. For example, recent research from MORI has shown that since 2002 the hitherto downward trend in the physical quality of the urban environment in many UK towns and cities appears to be reversing.[23] But the combination of social and economic forces, along with institutional responses to them, is creating an important tension. Public space in our towns and cities appears to be pulled by the magnetism of two contrary poles.

At one pole, the core ideal of public space – free and open access for all – is being undermined by a focus first and last on safety, which is creating bland, lowest-common-denominator spaces with no real power to draw or retain people. At the other, increasing diversity of lifestyles and culture is splintering public space into a patchwork of specialised monocultural enclaves defined by income bracket and identities of age, ethnicity and taste where people practice a 'mobility of avoidance' choosing to interact only with 'people like themselves'.[24] This bipolar pattern is played out in each of the cities we visited, and typified by the contrast between Callaghan Square and the Brewery Quarter in Cardiff.

Callaghan Square is one of Cardiff's newest public spaces, lying between the town centre and the Bay area. The large open square boasts a bloom of fountains, smooth marble benches and sloping stone floors. But it struggles to attract any people beyond office workers hurriedly cutting through on their way to work. Moreover, attempts by skateboarders to find a use for the expensive street furniture have been thwarted by the threat of a £100 fine and the addition, in the name of 'maintenance', of blocks and barriers that make it difficult to skateboard. In contrast, the Brewery Quarter just down the road bubbles with people even on a Tuesday night. The tight cluster of chain bars and restaurants organised around a small courtyard each have a distinct clientele who are served a bespoke mix of music, drinks and design aesthetic, from the Hard Rock Café to the Yard Bar.

Callaghan Square and the Brewery Quarter both seem a long way from the classical ideal of public space, and they highlight the continuing gap between its promise and the reality that most people experience. If public space is to effectively counter these negative trends and deliver on its social and democratic promise, then city planners and policy-makers need to find better, more subtle ways to develop the space between the lowest-common-dominator blandness of places like Callaghan Square and the extreme fragmentation of places like the Brewery Quarter.

This middle space is the place – part physical, part social and cultural – in which the promise of public space in the twenty-first century can be realised. It should be the focus of a new attempt to create forms of governance, principles of design and everyday rules of conduct and exchange that match people's needs and interests and foster social value. Animating this middle space will depend on developing a much richer, more fine-grained understanding of how people interact in public space in their everyday lives, their expectations of it and how they create value from the spaces where they live, work and socialise.

Some people are starting to develop this middle space for themselves. In each case study city we talked to people using what is available and defying the bipolar pattern. Far from being passive inhabitants, people are taking the initiative and creating shared spaces and experiences, often reaching beyond their usual circle of friends and family. We found people reclaiming privatised places for public activities and making new uses of old spaces. In the process they turned even the most unpromising of spaces into valued and shared places and experiences. In other words people are creating and recreating public space through their adaptive use of it.

One facilitator of this kind of activity is the Knowhere Guide, an open source encyclopaedia of UK cities. Started as a tool for skaters to identify good places to meet up with like-minded people and skate, the Knowhere Guide has expanded to include clubs, music venues and places to hang out. Visitors can log on to the site and post recommendations or access those made by others. One of the most prolific parts of the site is the section on 'hook-up spots', described as 'that hallowed spot where everyone hangs around with their mates dreaming of the time when they can get into the pubs or clubs – a bench, a corner: you name it.'[25] The listings identify these micro-sites ranging from pavilions and bandstands in local parks to knowing the right steps outside the right building. The postings include notices of when it's good to go, and warnings of when it is not, and what kinds of people you are likely to encounter.

Through this kind of ground level intelligence and energy, the three case studies revealed that some people are able to piece together a kind of network of both conventional and alternative public spaces for themselves. The purpose of this report is to help understand these kinds of everyday communities of interaction and participation better, and explore how this intelligence can be encouraged to 'trickle up' and reach a wider scale to encompass the whole urban fabric of a town or city. The next chapter sets out how people shape the spaces around them and considers the range of factors that constrain or expand the use of public space.

03. Start with the people not the space

If public spaces are to have a greater degree of traction as social, shared spaces, then the essential first step is to start with people rather than the physical space... Only with a much more sophisticated understanding of people's diverse values, motivations and needs will city planners be able to begin to identify what might provide the basis for either sharing spaces in common or negotiating differences.

Danny
is 20 and came to the city to go to university. He loves the place not least because it's got quite a few gay bars and clubs – well certainly more than where he grew up in rural Northern Ireland. He knows which places in the city it is safe to be outwardly gay and the places that aren't. When he is out at night the run to grab extra cash or a taxi home after a night out is always approached with some trepidation as it requires going through a square which is a 'really straight area'. (Cardiff)

Jeana is 78 years old and is having a coffee and a chat with her best friend in the supermarket café. She doesn't like going out on her own as she's worried about 'all the crime'. She doesn't have a car and doesn't dare use the bus because keeping up with the timetables is a bit of a challenge. She got dropped off at the supermarket by the dial-a-ride bus, which also picked up her friend. Her budget stretches to one or two trips a week on the dial-a-ride, which give her a regimented two hours before she's picked up again and taken home. Jeana is pleased with herself as she got her shopping finished early today and so has got time for a coffee. (Preston)

Geehta is in her early 30s with a well-paid job in research science. She moved to the town quite recently and is not too sure about where is good to hang out. She has struggled to find anywhere to go out that isn't dominated by alcohol, let alone anywhere that serves halal meat. She avoids the old part of the town because she's heard it can be unwelcoming if you aren't white. She finds herself either visiting other cities where she knows there are places she feels comfortable, or staying home and cooking dinner with friends. (Swindon)

Public space is a simple idea: a place for the public. However, people are complicated. No matter how wisely and imaginatively designers and architects create a public space, each person will interpret it differently and consequently use it differently – or indeed choose not to use it.[26] As discussed in the last chapter, public life is currently being squeezed between bland lowest-common-denominator spaces that fail to attract and retain people, and extreme balkanisation which fragments people into selective enclaves of income, gender, age and ethnicity. If public spaces are to have a greater degree of traction as social, shared spaces, then the essential first step is to start with people rather than the physical space and to understand the desire and capacity of different people to participate in the public spaces of their town or city. Only with a much more sophisticated understanding of people's diverse values, motivations and needs will city planners be able to begin to identify what might provide the basis for either sharing spaces in common or negotiating differences.

One of the aims of our research in Cardiff, Preston and Swindon was to help develop this kind of understanding. The field research comprised three stages. First, our interviews with representatives of local authority, community and business groups helped us to select five public spaces in each city where we interviewed people using them at different times of the day. Over 500 people were interviewed at this stage. We asked people about and recorded: why they were in the space; what they thought of it and how often they came; where else they liked to go in the city and how often; and what they liked and disliked about the city. Second, we ran nine focus groups (three in each city) with different social, ethnic and age groups.[27] The focus groups were important to ensure that we spoke to people who either rarely or never used public space as well as regular users. In the focus groups we asked people to identify the places they went to as part of their routine and places that were special to them in some way; and then the places they went where they mixed with people like themselves and places where they mixed with people unlike themselves.[28] A discussion was held around how people in the group used the spaces, what they thought of other people using them and what kind of activities they liked and did not like to see within them. From the focus groups we identified a list of conventional and less conventional public spaces that the groups considered to be shared in some way. In the third stage we selected 15 of these spaces (five in each city) to explore further. We interviewed the managers of the space (if there was one) and the users at different times of the day. We asked people the same set of questions we asked in the first stage.

At the outset of our research we had imagined that we would be able to characterise how people used space along the lines of age, gender, class and ethnicity. However, the field research illuminated the fact that people's perceptions, use and navigation of public space cut across these conventional categorisations. Instead, from the data we were able to identify ten broad types of public space user. These are not presented as an exhaustive and definitive typology. The range and type of public space users will be different in different cities. Instead, the typology is intended as a way to begin to sensitise urban policy-makers, city planners and other urban professionals involved to the diversity of the ways in which people interact with their environment. So far this kind of approach has been missing from much urban policy and practice, which has tended to focus on physical design, maintenance issues and centrally determined outcomes.

I don't get around much anymore. I like watching the telly at home. I like the cricket but I don't go to the stadium. I'm an armchair man.

White man, 65+, Cardiff

Mostly I go round friends' houses, or they come to mine. If you don't drink alcohol there's not much you can do here.

Asian woman, 20s, Swindon

Home Birds

Home Birds live cocooned lives. They rarely come into contact with public venues or public spaces. They centre their lives on their own homes, their work and essential tasks such as going to the supermarket. They tend to have low pride in their town or have lost it. Their significant places tend to be outside the boundaries of their hometown and centre on pleasant resorts or the homes of loved ones and family. Sometimes a Home Bird forms one part of a couple and has given all their public roles to the other person – such as shopping or socialising. In these cases the Home Bird tends to be male and elderly and their wife is the person in charge of their public life. Some Home Birds have their home-centred life forced on them. For example, a number of gay women we spoke to reported that there were few places where they can feel comfortable being 'out'. Equally, some Muslim people did not feel comfortable in alcohol-saturated town centres. A number of young black men avoided going out because they felt they had been hassled by the police once too often. These people are constrained into conducting their social life around their home or their friends' and families' homes.

Spaces and places Home Birds populate
Their own living rooms, kitchens and gardens and those of their friends and family.

Mall Walkers

Mall Walkers are not always elderly though they often are. They are not always female but they usually are. They include other groups such as some young mums and unemployed people. They often travel in pairs or small groups. What brings them together is their need to fight boredom and low self-esteem. They can frequently be found in shopping centres, department stores, fast food outlets and bus stops. Often they combine a trip to the supermarket with having a coffee with their friend in the store restaurant. They feel most comfortable in commercial space because it acts as a guardian in terms of providing services (toilets) and protection (from the elements and other people) and because it makes few demands on them. Other types of space such as the library or the park may be free, but require a more complex set of behaviours, commitments and permissions that they may not want to negotiate.

I meet my friend and go down to Morrison's, do our shopping and then sit down and have a meal. I know I shouldn't do it but it's cheap. You should see me in IKEA.
White woman, 65+, Preston

It's warm and comfortable. I can sit down and count my receipts and see how much money I have left.
White woman, 65+, Swindon

Spaces and places Mall Walkers populate
Bus stops, department store and supermarket coffee shops and markets.

'Hoodsters

I really like it here. I do nearly all my shopping here and don't go into town much. I know lots of the mums round here, we help each other out.
White woman, 30s, Swindon

I come here everyday. I like to sit and watch people. I don't really go anywhere else.
White man, 20s, Swindon

'Hoodsters stay in their own postcode and don't like to venture outside. However, unlike Home Birds they like the public spaces around their home and make high use of them – including shopping centres, religious centres and parks. 'Hoodsters can be on low or no income. They are often mums with young children. They usually know their neighbours and safety and familiarity are a high priority. 'Hoodsters can be mobilised around particular amenities, such as a post office or local park if under threat.

Spaces and places 'Hoodsters populate
Local parks, local parade of shops, mosque, church, coffee mornings.

I really like the air ambulance. You can tell they are trying to make Preston better for people.
British-Asian male, late teens, Preston

I'm proud to be a Swindonian. I'm just proud.
White woman, mid 50s, Swindon

Patriots

Patriots are born and bred in the town. They want to be proud of their town and feel personally implicated if it is criticised. They often have extended families living nearby. They tend to have a strong affiliation to a neighbourhood or series of neighbourhoods where they know the streets, corner shops, religious and community centres.

Patriots tend to fall into two types – Nostalgics or Optimists. There are a lot of older white people who are Nostalgic Patriots. They tend to be occupied by the past, which can limit their horizons as there is a limited (and declining) pool of people who can share their same social and economic memories. Heritage events or museums are one of the ways that they are able to make connections with other people. Optimistic Patriots tend to be younger and often from minority ethnic groups. Often their daily economic lives (newsagents, takeaways, restaurants) are a central part of the streets' visual and social landscape. They have a strong sense of loyalty to districts as well as the whole town. Intriguingly the Nostalgic Patriots don't see the similarities between themselves and the younger Optimistic Patriots (or vice versa), even though the lives of the latter echo many of the aspects of the life Nostalgic Patriots now hanker for.

Spaces and places Nostalgic Patriots populate
Clubs and hobby groups where they can maintain their interests/profession from the past such as conservative clubs, ex-service men's clubs, railway workers pubs, bingo, tea dances, hospitals, football grounds.

Spaces and places Optimistic Patriots populate
Neighbourhood places (mosque, school, shops), football grounds, sports facilities.

Displayers

Displayers use public space as their theatre. They prefer to be in town rather than in the confines of home. There are a lot of young males in this group, but the group also includes night-time revellers out on the town, skateboarders, bladers, joggers and street entertainers and evangelists. Everything about them – their dress, their body language, mobile ring tones – is designed to be expressive, often aimed at the opposite sex or to impress their friends. They can bring a liveliness to public spaces and leisure venues, but they are also associated with or suspected of breaking the rules, littering, crime and vandalism. They can make other people feel unsafe, and can be seen as territorial, though the latter is often to do with the Displayer's fear or lack of experience of other places in their town. They can appear anywhere as their purpose is to exchange information through display. They can be guerrilla-like in their tactics, finding unpromising corners of squares, parks and industrial estates to make their own. The problem is not everyone understands their language

I don't know their names but we've checked each other out. [pointing] I've seen him before, him, him, him, that kid there and her. My mate fancies that girl there.
White male, mid teens, Cardiff

We often hang out in the multi-storey car parks for shopping trolley wars or buy random things and beat each other up in the street. . . . There's not enough space for our energy.
[his friend drops his trousers at a passer-by during the course of the interview]
White male, late teens, Swindon

Spaces and places Displayers populate
Everywhere, but popular places include streets with clusters of bars, leisure and entertainment districts, park benches, skateparks.

I can't wait for Nandos to open.
British-Asian woman, 20s, Swindon

Every Saturday I bring my granddaughter to town and we go to McDonalds, then we have a walk about, have a coffee or a drink in Starbucks, then we go to ToysRus or the Early Learning Centre.
White man, 60s, Swindon

Brand Addicts

Brand Addicts are often full-time workers and have highly structured lives. One result of this is that their favoured places are often empty when this group is at work. They like to go to the cinema, bowling, restaurants, superstores, theme bars and the gym. They are concerned with symbols of success – the cool places to be seen and the right kind of car to get them there. They are very focused on venues and do not remember street names. The spaces that occur in between their destinations are perceived as irrelevant and at worst dangerous. They often travel by car. A lot of regeneration is targeted at this group and their leisure preferences. The place where they mainly meet new people or mix with people unlike themselves is at work, but they are also happy to mix with other people once inside their chosen venue. Some people aspire to be Brand Addicts or are Brand Addicts when they can afford it. Others are frustrated Brand Addicts, disappointed that their yearned-for brands are saturated in alcohol or don't serve their kind of food. Others are obliged to become Brand Addicts, for example some disabled people in wheelchairs are restricted to the mega-sized chain venues as they tend to be the only places physically accessible to them.

Spaces and places Brand Addicts populate
Chain pubs, clubs, bars, leisure centres and entertainment districts.

Bright Lights

Bright Lights are the newcomers to the city. They are enamoured with the bright lights, facilities, shops and job or cultural opportunities. They can find great advantage in the anonymity of a city compared to rural communities or smaller towns but enjoy the increased chance of meeting like-minded people. They tend to home in on obvious landmarks or newly regenerated areas in terms of where they spend their time and how they describe the town to other people. They travel more than other groups and can frequently be found at the train station or getting a bus across town. Bright Lights tend to be optimistic about where it is better than where they came from. Besides, they came – so they know they can always escape. They add a lot to a city and its public spaces because they represent the city's attractiveness to newcomers. They are also more likely to be accepting of disruptive behaviour in public space, and may themselves shift the socially accepted norms of the city.

Cardiff has got everything you could ever want – loads of bars, loads of places to go out.
British-Asian man, 20s, Cardiff

I'm from Ireland, it's terrible being gay there. Preston is pretty good compared to where I'm from. At least there's a scene.
White man, 20s, Preston

Spaces and places Bright Lights populate
Bars, clubs, café quarters, regenerated arts districts and quaysides, shopping malls, the landmarks of the city, and transport hubs.

Hobbyhorses

I come down the allotment most evenings, even in winter; there's always something to do.
White man, 40s, Cardiff

I love books. I've been here every week for the last five years. You come back here in three hours – I'll still be here.
British-Asian man, 60s, Preston

Hobbyhorses live for their non-work, non-family-based activities, either pursuing one hobby exclusively or revelling in trying their hand at a bit of everything. They can range from leisurely amateurs to individuals practised enough to reach near professional standards. They can be any age, ranging from kids DJ-ing, young executives doing a bit of acting on the side, or retired people working their allotment. Initially they like the safety of organised activities, such as an evening class, but once confidence is gained they are often quick to organise their own activities and events. They like to travel in groups and do it for social reasons as much as the hobby itself. They are comfortable pursuing their hobby with new people, as they know they already share a common interest, and can be very welcoming. However, their high standards can put others off.

Spaces and places Hobbyhorses populate
Further education colleges, arts centres, community centres, parks, youth clubs – anywhere with some spare space where they can congregate and practice their chosen hobby.

Urban Safarians

Urban Safarians deliberately go out and track down different places and types of places to consume. They like to mix the rough and ready with the glam and shiny; and like the idea of diversity even if they don't have so many friends of different cultural or ethnic backgrounds. They often have money and are university educated but not always. They are eclectic in their tastes, but tend to have a few favourite places that they think of as their locals even if they are not actually near where they live. They take pride in knowing their cities and generally want to share their knowledge and their city with other people. They can be snobby about branded places and Brand Addicts. Authenticity is their holy grail; new places are trophies.

We went out last night – went to all the new bars and that on the quayside. Then we went down Bute Town for some spit and sawdust places – the real Cardiff.
White man, 50s,
Cardiff

I like to go and see different things, what's going on. I've got my ticket already for the Opera House. . . . I'd rather live in London, where there is more to choose from, but Cardiff is getting better.
White man, 70s,
Cardiff

Spaces and places Urban Safarians populate
They could turn up anywhere, but generally favour places they can eat, drink or talk. Arts activities and anywhere offering ethnic distinctiveness are popular.

Public Spirits

Public Spirits read books on benches, collect conkers in parks and gaze at monuments. What ties them together is their ability to be themselves in public and to stand and stare. They are out and about come rain or shine. They are heavy users of traditional public spaces such as parks, squares and facilities such as libraries and art galleries and spend more time in them than most other people. They are very public spirited and are likely to intervene, or at least want to intervene, to stop anti-social behaviour such as people dropping litter or stealing flowers from parks. Public Spirits tend to come from either end of the social spectrum. Either they are short of money (students, homeless people) and choose the free activities associated with public spaces, or they are relatively affluent and educated and are looking for something more profound from public space, or perhaps are escaping from commercial space. Students can be important Public Spirits helping to re-populate space in the daytime when others are in full-time work.

I know everyone who comes in this park. [exchanges greetings with passing dog walker], I keep an eye on things..
White homeless man, 30s, Preston

If there was a bench there I'd sit there and watch the world go by. . . . I'd like to tell those girls to stop smoking, tell 'em what it will do to them, but I don't dare. A few years ago I might have.
White man, 65+, Swindon

Spaces and places Public Spirits populate
Parks, squares, galleries, libraries, arts centres, amenity associations (such as 'friends of the park' societies).

Choice and inequality

The picture that builds up from understanding the diverse types of public space user is of a fragmented urban geography with people segregated by activity and inclination. Some of this fragmentation comes from choice and self-definition. We have become familiar with the kind of fluid and voluntary patterns of self-definition popularised in style magazines where we are encouraged to define ourselves, all guided by a set of multiple-choice questions.

But we also need to understand how other factors influence people's self-definition because it is the dynamic interaction of internal self-perception and external resources that determines how people see themselves and how good their experiences of the public life around them are. This interaction of internal and external worlds creates sharp patterns of inequality and disadvantage: while some people, such as Urban Safarians, Public Spirits and Bright Lights, are highly mobile and can move confidently and freely around their cities, others, like Home Birds and 'Hoodsters, remain strictly contained and constrained by where they live or work.

Universal free and open access to public space remains the ideal that our cities aspire to. However, the evidence from Cardiff, Preston and Swindon reveals that free and open access and participation in the public life of cities is far more complex than simply the absence of an admission fee or membership restrictions. Three sets of issues seem to be important in shaping the patterns of inequality within cities: resources, social norms and individual values.

Resources

Different people have different stocks of knowledge, time and money, which together help shape their ability to access different spaces and places.[29] We found that young people in particular had a restricted mobility and knowledge of their cities and tended to frequent spaces near their home and school or the city centre at weekends. While this pattern is probably to be expected, their lack of experience of other neighbourhoods tended to generate fear. For example, one teenager from Llanishen in Cardiff told us, 'I'd never go to Ely. You get your head kicked in if you go to Ely', even though he later admitted that neither he nor anyone he knew had ever been to Ely and got their head kicked in. These perceptions seem to hold for many people into adulthood, with adults in each of the three case study cities citing various neighbourhoods as 'no-go areas'.

The length of time a person had lived in a place also impacted on their knowledge of where to go and what public spaces were available. For example, one newly arrived woman voiced her frustration that she got loads of free newspapers coming through her door telling every detail about what houses were for sale, but nothing about what clubs, activities and events were available. However, knowledge did not automatically increase with length of residency. For example, a number of Nostalgic Patriots who were long-time residents felt overwhelmed by the pace of physical change and regeneration in their town and chose to avoid these areas.

Working hours were cited as an issue in limiting some people's use of public space. In the focus groups when people mapped out the places they went to as part of their daily routine a shocked realisation of their limited geography frequently followed. As one man in his early 20s said, 'I just go from home to work, from work to home. God, my life is so small. I just don't have time for anything else.' Many people were aware of having a limited time-budget which they had to ration. Some were conscious that their decisions were shaped by various invisible structures at work in their city. For example, the relatively fixed timetables for work, school, faith activities and nursery all help to organise and segment people into separate activities and separate time geographies.

Financial resources also help to determine people's use of public space, with people rationing their use of certain areas according to their spending power. For example, one woman who lived in an outer suburb reported that she only ever went into the town centre when she had enough money in her purse and otherwise stuck exclusively to her neighbourhood. Others reported that they limited going out to one evening a week because it was too expensive otherwise, or used tactics like going to student nights, even if they were not students, so they could take advantage of the cheap drinks.

Social norms

Public spaces are regulated through unwritten social codes where subtle rules, signs and symbols convey whom a particular space is for and what behaviour is permissible.[30] Social norms operate at a variety of levels, from the city-wide level to the very micro-scale of particular neighbourhoods. In our research, the impact of social norms held by the wider society on shaping people's behaviour in public space was most clearly evident in the experiences of gay people. For gay people social 'norms' were not always enforced in subtle ways, but sometimes in violent, confrontational ways. Many of the gay people that we spoke to who had moved to Cardiff and Preston moved because they perceived the cities to be more cosmopolitan, open and tolerant than where they had lived previously. The presence of a university with many diverse students was cited as a factor in both cities in contributing towards a more tolerant atmosphere generally, and within the university districts in particular. Within the case study cities the gay people reported that they were conscious of what areas and venues were accepting of 'out' gay people and which were not. Responses included:

It's all full of lager boys. There is no way I can kiss my boyfriend in there.

White man, late teens, Preston

I can hold hands with my girlfriend in the middle of the day in my street because everyone is at work and so no one will see us and have a go. I've been stared at before, spat at before... everything.

White woman, 20s, Preston

People Make Places: growing the public life of cities

It's a chain. Everyone looks really straight in there, so I act straight.

White man, 30s, Swindon

The impact of the dominant social norms of society on people's use of public space was not limited to gay people. Similar issues were raised by people from BME backgrounds, women and older people in each of the case study cities.

Table 01

MOTIVATION + BEHAVIOUR

VALUE / MOTIVATION	PERSONAL PRIORITIES	PUBLIC SPACE USER TYPE
INNER DIRECTED	* SELF ACTUALISATION: LEARNING, PERSONAL DEVELOPMENT * COGNITIVE NEEDS: KNOWLEDGE, NOVELTY, BEAUTY	PUBLIC SPIRIT HOBBY HORSE URBAN SAFARIAN BRIGHT LIGHT DISPLAYER BRAND ADDICT
OUTER DIRECTED	* ESTEEM NEEDS APPROVAL, ACCEPTANCE, BELONGING	PATRIOT HOODSTER MALL WALKER HOME BIRD
SECURITY DRIVEN	* SAFETY NEEDS FREEDOM FROM FEAR	

Individual values

Values are principles that signify personal priorities. They influence intentions, which in turn influence behaviour. For example, a personal value held by an individual could be that 'the environment should be protected' and so this may motivate him or her to walk and cycle as much as possible; this in turn shapes which spaces he or she moves in and his or her interactions within them. Building on psychologist Abraham Maslow's 'Hierarchy of Human Needs', first developed in 1943,[31] Britain-based cultural theorist and practitioner Pat Dade[32] has developed a useful way to think about people's value systems. People tend to hold and are motivated by one of three sets of values: they tend to be inner-directed, outer-directed or security-driven. Table 1 sets out these values, the kinds of personal priorities they generate, and how the ten types of public space user our research identified correspond to these value systems.

Conclusion

Together, these three sets of concerns – resources, social norms and individual values – shape the ability and confidence with which an individual is able to access and use different spaces and places in a town or city. These are the raw materials from which the public life of towns and cities grows or shrinks. For the social and democratic promise of public space to be realised, public spaces need to engage and serve people equally and simultaneously in all their diversity of needs, aspirations, backgrounds and resources. To do this those involved in planning and creating public spaces need to understand the interactions between these three sets of issues. The next chapter explores the spaces in Cardiff, Preston and Swindon where we found these sets of issues coming together to create positive interactions and a dividend for the public life of the wider city, and from which learning for other public spaces and other towns and cities might be gleaned.

04 From public space to public experience

What made the spaces public was not their ownership status, physical design or aesthetic appearance. Instead, we found that a much better guide to whether a particular space is valued as a public space is whether it was actively used and shared by different individuals and groups. In other words, the publicness of a space is composed of the experiences that people are able to create within it. In this sense, public space is co-produced; far from being created by a planner, architect or council maintenance team, it is created by people's active participation and everyday use.

Jacob *practises his front wheel bunny hops at the council-installed skatepark near his house while his younger brother peddles wide circles around him. Their grandad looks on; he's recently earned the nodding respect of the local skater gang by taking on one of the ramps in his motorised wheelchair. Excitement ensues as grandad gives the kids some money to go and buy a Slush Puppy from the contractor-run café in the nearby leisure centre. Returning with an ice headache and a blue tongue, Jacob explains that at the weekend that they are going to the flashy new Excite Centre that boasts a wealth of high-tech games and sports activities. Grandad questions whether the privately run centre counts as a public space because it 'charges a small fortune to get in'. Jacob scrunches his face and booms, 'Of course it's public grandad, there's all sorts of people in there.'*

Where is the public life of our cities? In Cardiff, Preston and Swindon we asked people questions, listened to them and observed them in order to map and understand the patterns of movement and use that they etched on their cities. Tracking the full diversity of different types of people – from Mall Walkers to Urban Safarians – our search took us to some unexpected places. What made the spaces public was not their ownership status, physical design or aesthetic appearance. Instead, we found that a much better guide to whether a particular space is valued as a public space is whether it was actively used and shared by different individuals and groups. In other words, the publicness of a space is composed of the experiences that people are able to create within it. In this sense, public space is co-produced; far from being created by a planner, architect or council maintenance team, it is created by people's active participation and everyday use.

One important implication of this shift from a place-based to a user-led understanding of public space is that the universe of public spaces within a city expands – potentially dramatically – as people are able to create public experiences in a variety of settings – civic, public, private, and spaces that blend elements of all three. This is particularly important as it reveals the process by which a space, including those which are privately owned such as shopping malls and out-of-town shopping centres, might be co-opted for public ends.

This expanded universe of public space was evident in each of our case study cities, with people identifying a far wider range of spaces and places as public than the conventional stock of squares, parks and streets. Sometimes this creativity and adaptivity was a response to the poor quality of more traditional state-owned space, but even where the quality of this was high people still sought out and created new kinds of public spaces.

Hubs of public life

The following public spaces provided particularly strong examples of hubs of public life within their city. Some of the spaces are formally private, some formally public, others somewhere in between. What the spaces have in common is that their 'publicness' is created through the exchange and interaction of different people and different uses. The experiences created within them act as a shared resource, fulfilling individual needs in ways that would not be possible through individual action alone. A description of each space and examples of public experiences that people generate within them are outlined below.

The Car Boot Sale, Preston

The covered market in Preston is a huge Victorian cast iron structure that shelters 1700sq metres of market stalls. Open at the sides, there can be quite a chill in winter. It hosts a market three days a week and a car boot sale two days a week and is available for use by groups in the town for other community events. In the last year it has been used as the centrepiece of a Caribbean Carnival, a procession place for the Chinese New Year celebrations, and the finishing line for a marathon. Other than these set piece occasions, it is the car boot sale every Tuesday and Thursday when the space comes alive with the bustle of hundreds of bargain hunters. The diversity of different types of people coming together in one space is unrivalled in Preston. Student bohos flick through old records; elderly Prestonians chatter in groups; office workers enjoy the theatre of activity; Asian mothers hunt for bargains.

Public experience

- *Belonging*: people reported that there was a high incidence of bumping into people that they knew and people would stop for a chat; a high proportion also reported they were comfortable passing the time of day with people they didn't know. Regular stall-holders help create a familiar point of contact and people can easily share common interests and passions whether they be books, antiques or old records.

- *Novelty and surprise*: the car boot sale is different every day depending on what stalls are there and what goods are in. People liked the sense of exploration and that they might 'discover' something different.

- *Different Roles*: at the car boot sale there are no fixed roles: shoppers can become traders with relative ease. And the consumption is far from passive – successful treasure hunting requires knowledge and bartering is the norm.

- *Empathy*: visitors to the car boot sale enjoyed being able to see other people's belongings and possessions. Seeing other people's things gave them a portal into other people's lives which, short of actually walking into someone's home, they could not find anywhere else.

Chapter Arts Centre, Cardiff

A converted school in the western district of Canton, Chapter Arts Centre has been running since 1971. It is home to over 50 studios, containing everything from working artists and creative industries to after-school maths and yoga sessions. It also has exhibition and performance space and a cinema. Open from 8:30am to 11pm every day (bar Christmas and New Year), over 150 community groups use it over the year. The heart of the building is the central concourse: low-price café / restaurant by day, 'the best bar in Cardiff' by night. The concourse has a chameleon life, used as a part-time office by home workers tapping into the free wireless internet service, a meeting point/self-organised crèche for young mums, a meeting space for community groups, and a gathering point for middle-aged couples having a post film debrief and young Cardiff trendies hanging out.

Public experience

- *Tolerance*: a diverse community inhabits Chapter on a daily basis and most people we spoke to reported that this was one of the main reasons they liked it. Appreciation of diversity was accompanied by a high level of tolerance, including acceptance of types of people who were not tolerated in other parts of the city. For example, we spoke to a number of young adults with learning difficulties who said this was one of the few bars in Cardiff where they felt comfortable socialising. Equally, a group of middle-aged women said they positively liked the fact that odd characters often lounged on the sofa, admitting that outside Chapter they would probably regard the 'old boys' as nuisance street drinkers.

- *Sociability*: regulars cited Chapter as a place where they had made friends with other visitors, something they reported was fairly unusual in other public spaces. For example, one evening class leader reported that in contrast to the situation after her classes run elsewhere in the city, when people would leave as soon as the class finished, at Chapter she had got to know everyone and most people stayed on after the class to have a coffee and a chat.

- *Status and esteem*: Chapter manages to blend its neighbourhood social club role with a culture and consumption caché. It is the place to be seen if you are interested in the latest art house film or this month's most fashionable beer.

The University of the Third Age, Swindon

Swindon is not known for its great public or civic spaces. However, although public experiences have been squeezed from more conventional places, it seems that they have emerged resiliently in alternative form elsewhere. The University of the Third Age (U3A) is one such place. A network of learning groups for retirees, the Swindon branch is one of the largest in the country. Members self-organise discussion or social groups on topics they are interested in. Swindon U3A currently has over 35 groups ranging from digital photography and geomorphology to jazz and French conversation. Slightly guerrilla-like in their operating style, groups can pop up in people's homes, community centres or the spare room of public or private organisations, anywhere with spare space they can occupy. Once a month U3A members come together as a group for a meeting and guest lecture.

Public experience

- *Confidence*: the rationale behind the U3A is to share knowledge and learn new things. There is no established curriculum or restriction over topics groups should choose to learn about. People reported that they had tried things and developed skills in activities that they would never have thought of trying, such as tai chi. People also reported that they had dusted off old skills and become confident in using and sharing them with others.

- *Mutuality*: the U3A is entirely self-created. It depends as much on the people who attend the groups as on those who run them, with a fluid distinction between leaders and learners – everyone is a participant. There is a strong sense of mutual support, with members, for example, encouraging each other to try different activities and see what will work.

Pontcanna Allotments, Cardiff

The patchwork of allotments are on the western suburban side of Cardiff, flanked on one side by the busy Western Avenue and on the other by Pontcanna Fields. There about 35 plots on the site, which is open and has suffered from vandalism and arson on occasion. During the week it is mainly retired men who work the land. At weekends, and during the long summer evenings, they are joined by their children and grandchildren and in the last couple of years a new set of young foodies and green lifestylers, keen to grow their own organic produce, have joined the ranks. Part of the allotment is dedicated to a community project working with local residents, particularly BME residents, to grow their own food. Eclectic work parties of children, youths in hoodies, parents in saris and community activists are in the process of transforming their sizeable plot.

Public experience

- *Companionship*: the allotment provides a long-running community of amiable acquaintances for many of the plot holders; some have had a plot for a decade or more, valuing it as something of a haven from the ups and downs in their lives. Different generations also get the chance to come together and share time and a hobby.

- *Learning*: from preschool to post doc, learning at every level is a daily activity at the allotment. This includes neighbouring plot holders trading tips, old hands teaching newcomers, students from the nearby college conducting permaculture experiments, and children finding out about nature and where food comes from.

Coate Water, Swindon

Coate Water is a country park situated on the eastern side of Swindon where the town joins its rural fringe. The park has a catchment area that spreads across the whole town and the villages to the west, south and north. Many of the rural dwellers prefer the managed countryside of Coate Water to that of the surrounding Wiltshire wilds. People come to walk dogs, picnic, feed the swans, play crazy golf, go fishing, gaze at the lake, ride bikes, ride horses and admire the miniature railway. Besuited businessmen visiting Swindon have even been spotted hunting for treasure in a geocache hidden somewhere in the park. The park creates the space to host a range of different activities in close proximity to one another, but not in such away that one person's enjoyment of the space inhibits another's.

Public experience

- *Beauty*: for many people, Coate Water is where they get their daily fix of nature and they love the diversity of the park, which includes a nature reserve. Most users like to balance a sense of escape with proximity to other people and therefore safety.

- *Playfulness*: the park hosts many playful activities that different groups of people can easily join and leave. People said they joined in kick-abouts, shared a joke while feeding the ducks or threw frisbees back to other people playing in the park.

Morrison's Café, Preston

The café is situated inside Morrison's Supermarket on the outskirts of Preston, adjacent to a dockside redevelopment. The café is subsidised – the managers say they want it to add to the shopping experience rather than make money in its own right. Plenty of people pop in to use it regardless of whether they are going to do any shopping. Food is inexpensive, service is delivered promptly to tables and it is company policy that customers are never hurried or moved along. The café is a source of pride for people working at the store and people who use it voice considerable loyalty. The users reflect a broad cross-section of the people of Preston.

Public experience

- *Escape*: from bored children being dragged around the supermarket and parents tired of pushing the trolley, to office workers popping in for a coffee break, users of the café all saw it as a safe haven from the stresses of the last hour. The fact that the supermarket allowed people to stay for as long as they wanted added to this feeling of calm and respite.

- *Belonging*: Morrison's Café is a café of regulars. Many of the users make it part of their weekly routine to stop off for a coffee or a special treat of fish and chips on a Friday. People feel comfortable there and regular customers felt like they knew the staff and were welcomed in.

Harris Library, Preston

The Harris Library is housed in a grand Victorian building in the centre of the city in the same building as the city museum. The library spreads across two floors and three rooms arranged around the museum. On the top floor there are archives and current newspapers, and beneath it there is a learning centre where visitors can enrol for different courses. On the ground floor is the main throng of a modern library. People relax on sofas, chairs and stools around the library, sometimes reading, sometimes not. Others are busy punching away at keyboards or browsing the foreign language book section, while children amuse themselves in the play area.

Public experience

- *Curiosity*: the library provides a forum for people to learn about their locality. Beyond the basic displays of local history, the library also hosts information stalls for people to convey aspects of importance in the local community such as one focused on Chinese New Year.

- *Community*: people valued the library as a quiet refuge from the bustle of the city. Many people liked the fact that they knew that other people had come in for the same reason, even if they did not actually talk to them.

Bute Town Youth Pavilion, Cardiff

Bute Town lies between the main city centre and the redeveloped bay and is perceived by those outside it as being disconnected from both. It is one of the centres for Cardiff's BME population and has some of the highest levels of disadvantage in the city. The Pavilion is housed in an unpromising brick and metal building, but both around it and inside it there is a hive of activity all year with children and young people aged 8–24. It has a sports hall, pool room, kitchens, a DJ booth, dark room and a bank of computers. In the day it runs Connexions and other services to help young people over 16 to find employment or education opportunities. From mid afternoon until late at the weekends it becomes the social centre for the whole neighbourhood's youth population of all ethnic backgrounds.

Public experience

- *Performance*: the Pavilion provides a theatre for peer-to-peer performance. There is a mix of different kinds of spaces with different kinds of performance going on within them. Some spaces are noisy and very physical where young people hang out and play table sports, usually with MP3 players streaming into one of their ears. Other spaces offer a quiet space in which to do homework and send emails – often to friends in the same room.

- *Autonomy*: the ratio of adults to teens is low, with the latter often organising and running their own activities. Young people don't get told what to do, but they are given plenty of options.

- *Personal development*: the Pavilion has a health programme that has managed to make exercise and healthy eating cool and smoking uncool. It also has a popular leadership scheme whereby young people can train to become youth leaders.

Asda Wal-Mart, Swindon

On the northern outskirts of the town in a shopping park that mixes big box retailers with a library and water fountains, this Asda Wal-Mart recently lost its title as the biggest in Europe to a new store in East Manchester. As the competitive edge on price becomes ever slimmer, supermarkets are starting to find other ways of attracting consumers. This often involves building direct links with the community around them. For some supermarkets this may mean dispatching a team of staff to creosote the fence of a local scout hut, while for others it might mean letting charity fundraisers shake charity buckets in the shop. The Swindon branch of Asda Wal-Mart makes its car park available to community groups. Since the branch opened it has been used for fêtes, barbeques and fundraising events. It was even on the shortlist for an anti-foxhunting ban protest at the beginning of 2005. Inside, the café provides a safe and low-cost treat for low-income couples – young and old alike – and a child-friendly retreat for mums and their offspring.

Public experience

- *Comfort*: the aromas, the smiling faces at the counter, and unhurried atmosphere all create a relaxing environment for people to take a break.

Llanishen Skatepark, Cardiff

The skatepark is in the northern suburbs of the city in the grounds of a council leisure centre. It has a range of ramps and gets a decent write-up on one of the credible skate websites. The park is used by kids from the four schools in the area and sometimes skater tourists from other neighbourhoods. Younger kids tend to come after school and the older ones come later, some staying after dark when it is not too cold. There is an intricate etiquette of who gets what space on which ramp and when, as the boarders, bladers and bikers weave around each other. There tends to be a strict gender division: boys skate, girls chat and pretend they are not watching the boys.

Public experience

- *Performance*: the skatepark is first and foremost a space for people to perform for their mates and the opposite sex. For example, a number of the skaters we spoke to said they went home when the girls went home, as there was no longer a point to being there if the girls were not there.

- *Autonomy*: the skatepark provides a free space where skaters and observers can hang out with little interference from anyone else, particularly adults. Adults who do not disrupt the rules are, however, not unwelcome – as illustrated by the example of Jacob's grandfather.

Developing a framework for public experience

So what might a user-led framework for public space experiences look like?[33] The publicness of a space can be measured in terms of its ability to provide a platform for the creation of different types of experience by different people. We found that our ten types of public space user tend to be oriented towards one motivation category: some are more concerned with seeking experiences that give them a sense of security; others focus on seeking experiences that contribute to inner-directed needs such as self-development; and others on experiences that enable them to build esteem among their peer group. This spectrum of needs associated with each of these motivation categories (see table 1) seems a good basis from which to develop a framework to assess the public experience value of different spaces within a city.

Such an approach raises some important issues. First, for a public space to be effective as a social, democratic space of interaction for all, it needs to be able to offer something for inner- and outer-directed and security-driven people; if public spaces prioritise one kind of need, then people not motivated by that need will be inclined to stay away. The key question here is whether providing more personalised experiences to meet people's different needs can at the same time strengthen the shared life of an individual space, neighbourhood or city. Second, it offers a way of assessing whether certain needs or types of people are being under-served by the current provision of public space. For example, we found in Cardiff, Preston and Swindon a shortage of display space for young people, obliging them to carve it out for themselves on street corners and benches. Other people often found it hard to read their behaviour and so reacted with unease to their presence. Third, can spaces that are good at meeting one type of need be enriched to widen the range of experiences available there? The supermarket café was very good at providing a sense of security and belonging for Mall Walkers – a group that otherwise tended to be under-served in terms of public spaces. But what is the scope for building on this sense of safety in order to develop the space so it might host a wider set of experiences, such as learning or self-development, which Mall Walkers could feel more comfortable engaging in? Finally, how might public space users with low confidence in terms of participating in the public life of their cities, for example some Home Birds, be encouraged to take more risks and access a wider set of spaces and experiences?

Within the ten hubs of public life in Cardiff, Preston and Swindon, some spaces are clearly more public in that they are able to support a broader range of public experiences than other spaces. Preston car boot sale, Chapter Arts Centre and Pontcanna allotment are able to respond to a wide range of types of user, everyone from Mall Walkers and 'Hoodsters, to Public Spirits and Urban Safarians; and with this diverse range of users they are able to generate a corresponding wide range of public experiences including belonging, self-development and performance. Other spaces are able to respond to a more limited range of user needs and motivations. For example, the supermarket cafés tend to function primarily as spaces offering a sense of safety and belonging for lower-income and older Mall Walkers and Home Birds. The research also highlighted that some of these spaces,

such as Chapter, have a transformative quality, helping formerly timid Home Birds to become more confident and participate in risk-taking activities.

From the public life of spaces to the public life of cities

To broaden people's access to a broader range of public experiences it is unlikely that focusing on individual public spaces in isolation will be sufficient: the range of people's needs and motivations is simply too great. As well as enriching individual spaces, the mix of different types of spaces within a town or city and the connections and flows between them also need to be developed. In this way, the network of public spaces available within a town or city adds up to more than the sum of the individual parts. In Cardiff, Preston and Swindon the contrasts in the quality and character of their overall stocks of public space is striking, with clearly a very different common resource being created in each place.

Taking a user-led approach jolts us into recognising that the universe of public space is a potentially much bigger, much more diverse one than many conventional accounts of public space would suggest. People can create positive public experiences of everyday interaction just about anywhere. However, this does not amount to saying that public space is therefore so adaptable and flexible that city leaders do not have to worry about it. The comparative strengths of Cardiff, Preston and Swindon's overall stocks of public spaces to produce shared experiences warn against such complacency. The real implication is that there is a much wider set of opportunities and resources available to influence public experiences and public spaces for the better that so far are failing to be sufficiently drawn together. City planners and policy-makers need to develop an approach to shaping public space that simultaneously improves the micro-climates and spaces within which public experiences emerge and link them together so there is a much more powerful cumulative effect. Improving the micro-spaces and connecting them up and altering the patterns of experience within and between them is the urgent governance challenge for cities if their public life is to be rejuvenated for everyone and not just the well-resourced few.

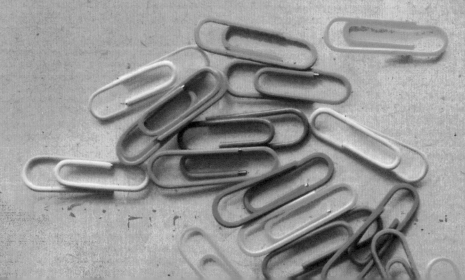

How shared are the public spaces?

To test the degree to which the public spaces in Cardiff, Preston and Swindon are shared we interviewed over 500 people in six public spaces – two parks, two civic spaces and two high streets or markets – in each town and city. Each person was asked to choose three words from a list of 24 that they thought best described the space they were in or how they felt when they were there. One-third of the words had a 'sharing' quality, for example: 'harmony' and 'friendly'. One-third of the words had an 'unsharing' quality, such as 'fear' and 'isolated'. One-third of the words were neutral. Combining the responses produced some striking results, with public space in Cardiff and Preston were perceived as significantly more 'shared' than that of Swindon.

Percentage of words selected that are 'sharing'

Percentage of words selected that are 'unsharing'

44% 43% 17% 15% 13% 33%

Cardiff Preston Swindon Cardiff Preston Swindon

05. The rules of engagement: design principles for growing the public life of cities

Reinvigorating the public life of our towns and cities requires improving the quality and range of public experiences available and the confidence and ability of people to access them. But the current set of tools for reshaping the public spaces of our towns and cities seems to be poor at meeting this reinvigoration challenge.

Reinvigorating

the public life of our towns and cities requires improving the quality and range of public experiences available and the confidence and ability of people to access them. But the current set of tools for reshaping the public spaces of our towns and cities seems to be poor at meeting this reinvigoration challenge. The emphasis on neutralising anti-social behaviour contributes little to encouraging social behaviour and may actually be diminishing people's confidence in the spaces outside their home. The reliance on iconic architects and their monumentalist designs seems to alienate as many people as it attracts and gives people little encouragement to break the habits of generally reserved behaviour in public spaces. And the focus of the liveability agenda in policy and practice on maintenance and cleanliness seems, at best, to represent only half the equation, with the social life of public space absent. What is missing is an understanding of how participation and interaction between people occurs and how it can be encouraged.

The ten hubs of public life identified in Cardiff, Preston and Swindon offer insight and learning about everyday participation and interaction from which we have developed a number of design principles for growing the public life of cities. It is from these 'rules of engagement' that other towns and cities seeking to increase the public experience value within their stocks of public, private and civic spaces might learn.

The rules of engagement

01. Access and availability

> *The door is always open from eight in the morning until 11 at night everyday of the year except maybe for five days – like Christmas. . . . . It's important that people can just walk through the door. They don't have to sign anything or show a card. It's a public space. No one is at the door saying 'hello can I help?' You know what 'can I help you means'; it means 'what are you doing here?' At Chapter people can just walk in and sit down. The only rule is that people have to manage and take responsibility for their own actions.*

> Janek Alexander, Director, Chapter Arts Centre

Most of the hubs of public experience were available either 24/7 (as they were open spaces) or had long opening hours. The best spaces were essentially 'on tap'. All the spaces were either free or were very low cost in terms of the activities or services on offer. The University of the Third Age had an annual membership fee of £18, but this was altered according to means. The annual charge at Pontcanna was about the same, and again discounts were available for certain groups. Bute Town Pavilion offers all its activities free of charge. ASDA, Morrison's and Chapter all subsidise their cafés and importantly all had a policy of letting someone make a cup of tea last all afternoon if they so wished. Significantly, it seemed that in a number of the spaces the amount of resources available to a group or an individual did not determine how much they could participate. In Chapter, the elderly gentleman nursing a subsidised cup of tea was as welcome and got as much value from the space as the young people at the next table enjoying pricey imported beer. Equally, at the car boot sale in Preston, those on subsistence incomes searching for bargains shared the space on a par with moneyed bohos rooting out old vinyls. Furthermore, while free access or minimal financial barriers to participation were an important consideration in people's choice to make use of a particular space, it was far from the only factor shaping their use.

Design principle into practice

Developing access and availability is a key issue for commercial spaces that often remain highly regulated during shopping time and often unused and inaccessible after closing time. The separation of commercial and civic life is artificial; the ancient agora was successful as a public space not because it was a political civic space – it was the market that drew people in. Now, retailers noting falling numbers in the mega malls are beginning to recognise the importance of deeper public experiences to attract people and get return visits. Selfridges, for example, have developed a programme of public art and cultural experiences as a core part of their offer. Similarly, the supermarkets we visited were putting on singles nights, wine tasting evenings and car park barbeques. Their experience shows that it is not a zero sum game; increasing civic and cultural activity is not necessarily at the expense of commercial activity.

- *Behaviour codes*: Speaking at a recent conference architect Ray Koon explained that when he designed the Bluewater Shopping Centre he created plenty of places for people to sit without having to buy anything. However, the management team running the shopping centre were quick to take these out.[34] Local authorities should integrate behaviour codes with the development of planning and design codes on new development to guarantee minimum space for non-commercial activity in new shopping malls. The Royal Festival Hall in London operates such a policy, where visitors are allowed to bring their own food into the Hall's public spaces and sit alongside people who have bought food from the outlets within the building.

- *Extended malls*: The Extended Schools initiative increases the role of schools in their communities by expanding their opening hours so that children can take part in more out-of-school activities and other community organisations can utilise school facilities. Like schools, shopping malls represent another under-used resource which could be 'extended' past their usual closing time. School may not be every child's favourite space, but for most it does feel secure and familiar; in a similar way, shopping malls play a significant role in the lives of many people we interviewed. Shopping malls could offer a safe and familiar environment for a range of additional activities, such as tea dances, art classes and other activities designed to appeal to currently under-served groups of people. Business Improvement Districts could take the lead on developing extended malls in partnership with local community groups.

02. Invitations: the importance of peer-to-peer evangelisers

Danny's late meeting his friends. Again. He's taking part in a tree planting youth project in a park, organised through his school. He's never been to the park before. When he exits the station he finds his friends have already gone on ahead. On the wall in front of him, there is a brown sign that forms the shape of an arrow, pointing to the right. It says 'Park'. He looks at it, pulls out his mobile and calls his friend. 'Hey Rob? How do I get to the park?'

Places cannot become public unless people know about them. They literally have to be publicised. A number of the hubs of public life outlined actively marketed themselves, for example, the U3A has a leaflet that it puts in libraries, and the market in Preston advertised in the local British-Asian press. However, those using these conventional methods reported a poor return. In getting people to come to a particular place, word of mouth is king and the messenger generally has to be someone who is known and trusted by the potential user. Repeatedly when we asked an individual why they had come to a particular place, they replied that a friend or family member had either brought them the first time, or had suggested they might like it.

Some of the spaces we visited had developed invitations into a sophisticated art. At Pontcanna, the Riverside Community Market Association is encouraging the local BME residents to use the allotments. Part of their strategy included hosting a picnic at the allotment on a sunny Sunday afternoon and using their personal contacts in the community to invite people and spread the word. At the Chapter Arts Centre, they have deliberately stretched the organisation's mission to include running an after-school maths club. The reasoning is that it is incredibly popular with the children in Cardiff's Chinese and Somali communities, and if they can get them into the building for maths the children or their parents might just like the look of something else that is going on there too.

Design principle into practice

- *'useyourtown.com'*: 'useyourtown.com' would be an Amazon-style website tool aimed at residents rather than tourists. Using collaborative filtering technology the site would offer personalised recommendations of places and spaces that the user might like, for example 'if you liked this, you might like this; for something different try this'. 'useyourtown.com' would personalise and humanise conventional listings magazines and be built out of the knowledge of a much wider population than a few 'expert' reviewers. 'useyourtown.com' could be built by the local authority, but its design should be as open source as possible, allowing anyone using the site to update and add comments.

03. *Exchange-based relationships*

> *I'm good at growing leeks. Probably too good – got hundreds of them. But that's alright coz I'll swap them with someone else who's got too much of whatever they're growing. . . . If someone wanders in from the park, then more likely than not they'll end up having a chat with someone and leave with an armful of something to take home.*

> White man, 50s, Pontcanna allotment, Cardiff

Interaction based on clear and purposeful exchanges between people is important in creating spaces where people feel comfortable. In the street interviews we conducted in Cardiff, Preston and Swindon we found that people felt commercial settings such as high streets and markets were more shared than civic squares or parks. This can be explained in terms of these being settings where interactions between other people are easily brokered through well-known rules such as queuing, choosing goods and paying for things. The literature regarding public space can be dismissive of this consumer-based exchange; however, it is an important part of people's lives and often their identities. It also reveals the importance of exchange relationships, which other spaces could emulate. These need not be financially based. The ten spaces our research identified were all good at fostering non-financial exchange relationships of one kind or another, including exchanges based on trading knowledge, skills and goods. For example, at the skatepark young people traded gossip and tricks; at the allotment, people traded gardening tips and produce; at the University of the Third Age people traded skills and knowledge.

It should be noted that not all exchange has to take place through practical activities. A common theme among many of the people we interviewed was how good some spaces were for watching people. Far from being a passive activity, people-watching provides a vital flow of information about a person's fellow citizens – who they are, what they are doing and what they look like. Many people said they enjoyed watching people because of the diversity of people coming and going.

Design principle into practice

- *Street swap*: Twinning with a city in another country has become common place among British towns and cities, with exchanges between schools, arts groups and businesses popular. But what about exchanges between different neighbourhoods within a city? Some people are more likely to visit Central Park in New York than a district within their own town. Street swaps could involve arts festivals, school link-ups and street games. Community-based organisations could take the lead in organising street swaps, with Local Strategic Partnerships encouraging whole-city networking.

04. Visible and invisible choreography

Interaction and conviviality are not automatic features of most public spaces. We found that balancing and responding to different users' needs sometimes requires a good deal of choreography on behalf of the official or unofficial guardians of a space. Sometimes this was obvious. ASDA for example puts its most outgoing and friendly 'co-worker' on the door to welcome people. Similarly, at the Harris Library an attendant is standing at the door to welcome people to the building, direct them to where they want to go, and also inform them about the contents of the museum and the temporary exhibitions in the art gallery housed in the same building. Sometimes it is less visible. For example, Chapter operates a complex system of supply chains, as their director explains:

> We move around different people and groups. Someone might come in to sing, someone will see her and suggest she tries out for a performance, or join so and so group. There are lots of separate activities that go on here at any one time. We don't want it to be a mush of everything the same. But people come in from a certain angle, we help put links in the chain and make introductions. We have 50 staff and they all have this as part of their role – from the security guy, to the woman on the front desk, to the curator, and of course me.

At Bute Town the 'choreographers' have also been at work. The Pavilion used to be used just by boys and young men, even though it was officially open to all. The team who run it have slowly encouraged more girls to attend and join in the activities by making certain times and activities female only. The result has been that more girls now use the Pavilion at all times of the day.

Design principle into practice

- *Dial 311 for public life*: Community groups and the formal or informal stewards are best placed to act as choreographers for individual spaces as they will be closer to the user groups, but choreography can also be enhanced at a city-wide level. In New York, City Hall has introduced a 311 telephone service as a clearinghouse for all non-emergency services and queries. When it first began operating the calls were about noisy neighbours, parking rules and fly-tipping. A year ago it was upgraded to become a one-stop shop for culture and entertainment advice, including alerts and information on street festivals, concerts and other public events. In its first year its operators handled over ten million calls. The service is funded by a mix of bodies: the council, local business and cultural institutions. Other cities could develop a similar service for their area and also offer text message alerts about upcoming events.

05. Leaving room for self-organisation

In many of the spaces that we visited, the division between the user and the authority controlling the space is blurred. This way users are encouraged to create activities for themselves and other users. For example, at the car boot sale, people pitch up with their car or stall and rent a space for just an afternoon or every week; at Coate Water a number of local groups run activities in the park – including a model railway and boating; at the University of the Third Age, anyone can start a group and as a result there is an ever-changing menu of clubs and activities; the Harris Library makes space available for community groups to come in and run information stalls; at ASDA Wal-mart, the car park is available to local groups for fêtes and other community activities.

Design principle into practice

- *Resources for activity*: More flexible approaches to 'planning gain' than conventional one-hit council-controlled Section 106 agreements are currently being developed. These include the proposed 'roof tax' to fund expansion in Milton Keynes where developers will be expected to pay a levy of £20,000 per new house, to be used to build schools, hospitals, roads and other facilities. A similar approach could be adopted in other new-build areas and a proportion of the fund could be set aside for community-led public realm projects and events. This could be important for place-making and building a sense of belonging in new communities. If the fund was set up as an investment fund with, for example, a development trust to manage it, the money could bring ongoing benefits to the local community.

- *Easy DIY*: In some cities it is easy to organise a street or music festival; in others, people's energy gets lost in a mess of regulations and bureaucracy. Local Strategic Partnerships could coordinate a review involving all the agencies that have a say in making a festival possible (police, transport, licensing, park authorities) and establish simple common ground rules and a presumption in favour of festivals going ahead.

06. Diverse activities encourage diverse people

It's early evening in the town centre and happy hour is drawing to a close in the Revolution Bar. A man who we later discover is a poet is leaning into a pile of freshly consumed alcopop bottles. He urges us to talk to him.

> *'What are you doing in Swindon? Why are you doing researching HERE? Why don't you go somewhere decent?' He starts to shout. 'IT'S RUBBISH HERE!' 'There are other places in Swindon that are good but this whole area is terrible. I've been away. I've come back: AND IT'S THE SAME. It's the people, they're so . . . they're all like each other. They're all THE SAME!'*

In Cardiff, Preston and Swindon, the places that struggled tended to be the spaces where only one type of activity or one type of user participated. In all three cities the emergence of spaces saturated with bars was highly prohibitive for those who were not young and with a keen thirst for drink. The ten hubs of public life identified in the previous chapter were able to encourage a mix of different kinds of activity. People tended to feel more uneasy or even threatened when a space was dominated by one group of people engaging in one type of activity than when two or three distinct groups were engaging in different kinds of activity. For example,

Preston car boot sale, Chapter Arts Centre and Coate Water hosted lots of different ways for people to interact within the space and this encouraged a broader range of people. The car boot sale was able to attract people struggling to make ends meet, specialist collectors, people out for the thrill of a bargain or people just enjoying the spectacle during a lunch break. More generally, by programming carnivals, festivals and other community activities into the space when not functioning as a market or car boot sale, the covered market area was able to attract a variety of different visitors throughout the year.

Design principle into practice

- *Public experience audit*: A local authority-led audit of the quality and range of public experiences within its area would help identify the relative strengths of particular spaces and inform a view of the overall quality of the city's public space network. For example, the management of a particular park might be good at providing security, but poor at supporting learning or performance activities. The audit could help to prioritise funding. For example, the audit might identify that certain groups are poorly provided for in terms of the types of experience they can access, such as performance space for young Displayers.

- *Reclaiming the night-time economy*: The combination of liberalising drinking hours and cracking down on drunken behaviour are unlikely to solve the binge drinking problem in town centres. The problem originates in the concentration of drinking establishments and the lack of any other type of activity on offer. Cities need to give other people reasons to be there to break up the monoculture. Alongside liberalising the drinking hours, cities should also seek to liberalise the hours of shopping, public buildings, museums and libraries so that there is a genuine diversity of activities on offer. This would require joint working between the public institutions and local businesses, perhaps as part of a Business Improvement District.

07. Networked space

> We walked here [Pontcanna allotments] from the farmers' market this morning. Yes I made my children walk. We walked across the big field and my son saw a horse for the first time in his life.
>
> *Somali woman, 30s, Cardiff*

A number of the spaces identified as hubs for public life did not just operate in isolation and instead consciously linked themselves and their users to other spaces within the city and sometimes beyond, contributing vitality to wider networks of public space. For example, Riverside Community Market Association helps run a farmers' market on the edge of Cardiff city centre and is planning to produce and sell vegetables grown at the allotments at the market. A number of stall owners from the market are also involved with working on the community allotment. At the University of the Third Age in Swindon, there are a number of music or dance groups that have put on public performances in community centres and at festivals.

Design principle into practice

- *Network audit*: For the stocks of public spaces within a city to add up to more than the individual sites, connectivity is vital. Cities are shaped as much by the quality and quantity of the flows of people, information and goods between different places as by the individual places themselves. To understand these flows and the connections and disconnections they create, local authorities should lead a process of 'flow mapping' within their area. This would include analysing flows such as patterns of investment, transport movements, new residents and business arrivals which help shape the physical network of spaces and places.

- *Urban safaris*: To help build up people's confidence, knowledge and mobility, cities should promote safaris within their borders. The safaris could be targeted at particular groups that have lower confidence and mobility in their cities, such as Home Birds and Mall Walkers. Equally, the safaris could be used to promote activity and encourage different user groups to come at particular times of day in parts of the city that are under-used – for example the 5–8pm evening economy. Tourist authorities working in collaboration with community or service organisations and their clients and members could develop this in-city tourism.

08. Props and permission

If someone said hello I'd be friendly back.

Asian-British man, 40s, Cardiff

I'll say hello to the other people who walk their dog here even if I don't know them.

White man, 20s, Cardiff

I'll talk to someone if they talk to me first.

White woman, 50s, Preston

I'm a bit shy, so I guess I use my kids a bit to help me meet people.

White woman, 30s, Swindon

It's actually quite nice to a have a stranger come up and talk to you.

White woman, 65+, Swindon

The default position of most people in public spaces seems to be that of pursuing private activities (walking, reading, talking) either as an individual or as part of a group that has a pre-existing relationship (friends, family etc). When users of a public space have a sense that other people appear to have a reason to be there, for example walking a dog, taking children out or painting a picture, they tend to be more comfortable sharing a space with them. These kinds of props (dogs, babies, small children) make people feel more comfortable and importantly help people interact. Get the prop right and people feel they have permission to engage in more public, social behaviour. The spaces identified in Cardiff, Preston and Swindon as hubs of public life tended to be prop-rich or encourage people to bring their own. For example, Coate Water provides a host of props in the form of a railway, ducks in the pond and wildlife walks. It is also a place to which people tend to bring props in the form of dogs and children.

Design principle into practice

- *Bringing life to the liveability agenda*: The liveability agenda and spending tend to focus on maintenance and cleanliness issues. Important as these factors are for making pleasant neighbourhoods, liveability also needs to embrace sociability. Aside from the mega-sites of grand squares and regenerated quaysides, the next strategic sites for cites looking to grow their public life are the everyday spaces of the local neighbourhood and the micro-sites within town centres and parks: outside shop doors, benches at bus stops, recycling points and market stalls. Public art, or information targeted for different public space users who use these spaces could be encouraged. One simple and low-cost idea would be for local authorities to create a series of 'talking benches'. One bench in every park or street could be designated for chatting; if you sit down it means you are happy to pass the time of day with whoever sits down next to you.

09. Safety: last, but not first

We used to have security guards in the entrance, but then we realised that they just made people edgy. They actually encouraged people to look for trouble. We now put our best, outgoing friendly co-workers on the door to greet people as they enter, which works a big improvement. Customers feel secure, but in a better way.

Manager, ASDA Wal-mart, Swindon

For many, safety is the cornerstone on which public space rests. Fear is the undoubted enemy of public experiences. This concern, however, often results in safety dominating the design of public spaces with watchful television cameras, security guards and anti-climb paint as baseline requirements. However, the example above articulates a common sentiment among all the people and places we visited. A sense of safety is encouraged more through developing social behaviour than by focusing on regulating anti-social behaviour out of existence.

The research suggested that things like better lighting and fewer bushes were a key concern of some visitors to public spaces, but the kind of sense of safety that might change people's behaviour and result in them using different spaces for a wider range of activities, came more from a combination of the other 'rules of engagement' described above. People were more likely to talk about safety concerns when public places were empty, when there was no easily accessible, approachable guardian for the space, or when they were dominated by one group of people, or when they had little say in what happened in them. Knowing that there is somebody to talk to if you have a problem or an enquiry (like a park ranger), that there are people who give you permission to enter a space (welcomers and 'choreographers') and that there is a range of people conducting a balance of different activities gave people a more compelling sense of security than attempts to isolate and neutralise anti-social behaviour.

Conclusion

Growing the public life of towns and cities is not an agenda to be held and controlled by town planners and architects alone. It will require action from central government and local authorities as well as civic and community organisations, and commercial developers and businesses such as supermarkets and shopping centres. However, any action will be effective only if it is done with the everyday collaboration, participation and leadership of people, the users themselves.

06.
Conclu-
sion

The challenge for cities is to learn from the micro public spaces that are proving to be effective platforms for shared experiences – from car boot sales and allotments to supermarket cafés and art centres.

People Make Places: growing the public life of cities

TRUST

The dominant urban narrative for the past 25 years has been a tale of the progressive privatisation of the communal spaces in our towns and cities wherein the space for shared experiences has got smaller and more fragmented. The challenge now is to find a new story that reconnects these spaces – public, private and civic alike – and to grow anew the shared life of our towns and cities. This agenda applies as much to a neighbourhood park as it does to an out-of-town shopping centre.

In Cardiff, Preston and Swindon we found spaces that are hubs for public life, where people are able to create shared experiences and play an active role in animating the space. The publicness of these spaces is created by the interaction of people and their environment and would be impossible without people's everyday participation. Far from being delivered in isolation by an architect's design brief, or the council's maintenance team, these public spaces are co-produced.

This process of co-production holds out a potentially powerful way forward in terms of closing the persistent gap between the promise and reality of public space. It is adept at countering some of the negative trends that are perceived to be undermining public space as well as working with the grain of these trends and creating positive externalities.

First, co-production helps to counter the decline in trust in other people's behaviour and to generate a sense of community efficacy. Our research found that across age, gender, ethnic and class differences people tended to be quite conservative about what kinds of behaviour from other people they were comfortable with in public spaces.[35] Concerns about safety and certainty were frequently voiced in the street interviews and focus groups we conducted. Where the organisation of the spaces reflected the principles of co-production, however, there tended to be a much higher confidence in other people's behaviour and greater openness to a diversity of activities and people; people felt safe, but were more willing to take risks, for example by talking to people they did not know or trying a different kind of activity. The mix of easy exchange between people and the fact that people felt they had helped create what was going on in the space helps build up their trust of other people.

Second, by drawing on the diversity of people in the creation of shared experiences, co-production helps spaces to avoid the twin dangers of a lowest-common-denominator blandness or extreme fragmentation. Because co-produced spaces are partly self-organised they tend to be much more flexible, responsive and therefore more able to simultaneously meet a diversity of needs. Inclusion is achieved but not at the cost of blandness, as the steward of one public space describes, 'Here it's not a bland mush of integration where everything is the same. It's somewhere where different people can come and do their thing and maybe rub up against each other, interest and even inspire them.'

Third, co-production is governance-neutral and can work in a range of environments – public, private and civic – to improve their quality. Public space works best where people are able to positively contribute to their everyday environments through their personal choice and actions. The implication for governance of every type of space – public, private or civic – is that more space and control needs to be given over to the people using it. This process of 'letting go' could also be the means by which different types of spaces are better connected together.

Revitalising the public life of cities demands that we start with people rather than with physical space. It rests on a much richer understanding of how people interact in public space in their everyday lives, their expectations from it and how they create value from it. The challenge for cities is to learn from the micro public spaces that are proving to be effective platforms for shared experiences – from car boot sales and allotments to supermarket cafés and art centres. This learning should inform efforts to put in place the structures and resources to enable the ground level energy to trickle up and reach critical mass across the whole urban fabric. Moreover, if this 'public space from below' can be effectively harnessed it may well hold some wider democratic lessons for other institutions searching for a way to reconnect with people and their everyday lives.

Notes

Notes

1   For the purposes of this report, although Cardiff and Preston officially have city status and Swindon doesn't, there are significant arguments for treating it as a city as expressed in its failed applications for city status – most recently in 1999 and 2002. For the sake of simplicity and readability, we have referred to it as a city.

2   J Goss, 'The "magic of the mall": an analysis of form, function and meaning in the contemporary retail built environment', *Annals of the Association of American Geographers* 83, no 1 (1993).

3   S Johnson, *Emergence* (London: Penguin, 2001).

4   R Trainor, 'The middle-class' in P Clark (ed), *The Cambridge Urban History of Britain* (Cambridge: Cambridge University Press, 2000).

5   JK Walton, 'Towns and consumerism' in Clark, *The Cambridge Urban History of Britain*.

6   Trainor, 'The middle-class'.

7   C Segal, 'Greek tragedy and society' in JP Euben (ed), *Greek Tragedy and Political Theory* (Berkeley: University of California Press, 1988).

8   R Sennett, *The Fall of Public Man* (London: Faber, 1986).

9   M Sorkin (ed), *Variations on a Theme Park: The new American city and the end of public space* (New York: Hill and Wang, 1994); D Mitchell, *The Right to the City: Social justice and the fight for public space* (New York: Guilford Press, 2003).

10 See, for example, *Living Places* policy document series (Office of the Deputy Prime Minister).

11 Performance and Innovation Unit, *Social Capital: A discussion paper* (London: PIU, 2002), p39; available at: www.strategy.gov.uk/downloads/seminars/social_capital/socialcapital.pdf (accessed 13 July 2005).

12 Commission for Architecture and the Built Environment (CABE) Space, *The Value of Public Space* (London: CABE Space, 2004); see also: www.cabespace.org.uk/policy/reports.html (accessed 13 July 2005).

13 M Power, *The Risk Management of Everything* (London: Demos, 2004).

14 D Rowe, 'The assessment of risk is a very personal thing', in CABE Space, *What are we Scared of? The value of risk in designing public space* (London: CABE Space, 2005).

15 T Bentley, *Letting Go: Complexity, individualism and the left* (London: Demos, 2003).

16 M Hajer, *In Search of the New Public Domain* (Rotterdam: Nai Publishers, 2002).

17   ODPM, *Cleaner, Safer, Greener* (London: HMSO, October 2002).

18   CABE Space, *The Value of Public Space*.

19   C Shearing and J Wood, 'Nodal governance, democracy, and the new "denizens"', *Journal of Law and Society* 30 (September 2003); available at: http://papers.ssrn.com/sol3/papers.cfm?abstract_id=437762 (accessed 13 July 2005).

20   R Florida, *The Rise of the Creative Class and how it is transforming work, leisure, community and everyday life* (New York: Basic Books, 2002).

21   ODPM, *Investment in 'Quality of Place' and Regional Economic Performance* (conference paper) (London: ODPM, 2005).

22   CABE Space, *The Value of Public Space*.

23   CABE Space, *Parks and Squares; Who Cares?* (London: CABE Space, 2005).

24   Hajer, *In Search of the New Public Domain*.

25   See: www.knowhere.co.uk (accessed 13 July 2005).

26   Rowe, 'The assessment of risk is a very personal thing'.

27   In each city we conducted three focus groups: one gay, lesbian and bisexual group aged 18–40; one BME group aged 18–30; and one group with participants aged over 65. All the groups were 50% male, 50% female.

28   Participants were asked to decide for themselves what 'different from myself' meant.

29   P Adams, 'A reconsideration of personal boundaries in space–time', *Annals of the Association of American Geographers* 85, no 2 (1995).

30   L Lees (ed), *The Emancipatory City: Paradoxes and possibilities* (London: Sage, 2004); K Namaste, 'Genderbashing: sexuality, gender and the regulation of public space', *Environment and Planning D: Society and Space* 14 (1996); N Fyfe, *Images of the Street: Planning, identity and control of public space* (London: Routledge, 1998); B Gleeson, 'Justice and the disabling city', in R Fincher and JM Jacobs (eds), *Cities of Difference* (New York: Guilford Press, 1998).

31   AH Maslow, 'A theory of human motivation', *Psychological Review* 50 (1943).

32   Demos interview with Pat Dade, 8 June 2005.

33   A number of thinkers and institutions are beginning to tackle the issue of more user-led approaches in other areas of public investment and the delivery of public service and public goods. One of the most influential conceptual frameworks currently is that of 'public value', first developed by Harvard academic Mark Moore. Put simply, public value is 'what the public values: what it is prepared to give time, money or freedom for'. It is a multidimensional concept that incorporates the conventional sense of economic

value but also takes into account a set of softer social values such as fairness, equity, trust and sustainability. It is beginning to be applied to some areas of public service reform. For example, the BBC recently embraced it as the organising concept for its charter renewal process.

34　R Koon speaking at the conference, 'Belonging and Identity in New Neighbourhoods', British Urban Regeneration Association and Church in Society, Chatham, Kent, 16 March 2005.

35　We tested a number of 'rules' in our nine focus groups and recorded the responses. Overall, the different groups agreed with the following rules: dogs should be kept on leads at all times except in large parks; busking should not be encouraged as it is associated with begging; barbeques should be allowed only in regulated spaces and only if they are not too smelly; children should not be encouraged to play in the street; it is strange to see two men holding hands in the street; homeless people should not be allowed to sleep in the park. Overall, the group most open to different kinds of behaviour in public were the BME 18–25 group in Preston; the most closed, the gay group in Swindon.

Data table

36　All peer and aspiration towns and cities were identified by local stakeholders during interviews in the case study town and cities.

37　2001 Census, Distribution of the population of Wales by local authority area: 1981, 1991 and 2001; available at: www.wales.gov.uk/keypubstatisticsforwalesfigures/content/population/2003mye-la.htm (accessed 13 July 2005).

38　2001 Census, Usual resident population: key statistics for local authorities; available at: www.statistics.gov.uk/StatBase/ssdataset.asp?vlnk=6555&Pos=1&ColRank=1&Rank=224 (accessed 14 July 2005).

39　Ibid.

40　Based on Audit Commission assessments of ten Cardiff County Council services between 2002 and 2004.

41　Audit Commission, *Comprehensive Performance Assessment Report, 2003/04* (London: Audit Commission, 2003), see also: www.audit-commission.gov.uk/cpa (accessed 13 July 2005).

42　Audit Commission; see: www.audit-commission.gov.uk/authority.asp?CategoryID=ENGLISH^576^LOCAL-VIEW^AUTHORITIES^108202 (accessed 13 July 2005).

43　2001 Census, Ethnic group: key statistics for urban areas, summary results for local authorities; available at: www.statistics.gov.uk/StatBase/ssdataset.asp?vlnk=8296&Pos=1&ColRank=1&Rank=240 (accessed 15 July 2005).

44　Office for National Statistics; available at: www.wales.gov.uk/keypubstatisticsforwales/content/publication/economy/2004/sb42-2004/sb42-2004.htm (accessed 13 July 2005).

45　Preston City Council, August 2004.

46   Swindon Chamber of Commerce and Industry, 'Travel Patterns to Work for Swindon' (2003).

47   See www.cardiff.ac.uk/about/facts/index.html (accessed 13 July 2005).

48   Higher Education Statistics Agency, *Higher Education Management Statistics 2003/04* (Cheltenham: HESA, 2004).

49   www.gay2z.com (accessed 13 July 2005).

50   www.cardiff.gov.uk/ (accessed 13 July 2005).

51   2001 Census, Age structure: key statistics for local authorities; available at: www.statistics.gov.uk/ StatBase/ssdataset.asp?vlnk=6556&Pos=2&ColRank=1&Rank=224 (accessed 15 July 2005).

52   Ibid.

53   www.cardiff.gov.uk/ (accessed 13 July 2005).

54   2001 Census, Age structure: key statistics for local authorities.

55   Ibid.

56   Welsh Indices of Multiple Deprivation 2000, available at: www.wales.gov.uk/keypubstatisticsforwales/ content/publication/social/2001/sb13-2001/depscores-md2000.pdf (accessed 13 July 2005).

57   Indices of Deprivation 2004, ODPM, available at: www.odpm.gov.uk/odpm/SOA/LASummaries2004.xls (accessed 13 July 2005).

58   Ibid.

59   2001 Census, Economic activity – all people: key statistics for local authorities; available at: www.statistics.gov.uk/StatBase/ssdataset.asp?vlnk=6567&Pos=2&ColRank=1&Rank=224 (accessed 15 July 2005).

60   See: http://news.bbc.co.uk/1/shared/spl/hi/in_depth/uk_house_prices/counties/html/county13.stm (accessed 13 July 2005).

61   ONS, New Earnings Survey 2003, p107; available at: www.statistics.gov.uk/downloads/theme_labour/ NES2003_GB/NES2003_Streamlined_analyses.pdf (accessed 13 July 2005).

Demos – Licence to Publish

THE WORK (AS DEFINED BELOW) IS PROVIDED UNDER THE TERMS OF THIS LICENCE ("LICENCE"). THE WORK IS PROTECTED BY COPYRIGHT AND/OR OTHER APPLICABLE LAW. ANY USE OF THE WORK OTHER THAN AS AUTHORIZED UNDER THIS LICENCE IS PROHIBITED.   BY EXERCISING ANY RIGHTS TO THE WORK PROVIDED HERE, YOU ACCEPT AND AGREE TO BE BOUND BY THE TERMS OF THIS LICENCE. DEMOS GRANTS YOU THE RIGHTS CONTAINED HERE IN CONSIDERATION OF YOUR ACCEPTANCE OF SUCH TERMS AND CONDITIONS.

1. Definitions

a. "Collective Work" means a work, such as a periodical issue, anthology or encyclopedia, in which the Work in its entirety in unmodified form, along with a number of other contributions, constituting separate and independent works in themselves, are assembled into a collective whole. A work that constitutes a Collective Work will not be considered a Derivative Work (as defined below) for the purposes of this Licence.

b. "Derivative Work" means a work based upon the Work or upon the Work and other pre-existing works, such as a musical arrangement, dramatization, fictionalization, motion picture version, sound recording, art reproduction, abridgment, condensation, or any other form in which the Work may be recast, transformed, or adapted, except that a work that constitutes a Collective Work or a translation from English into another language will not be considered a Derivative Work for the purpose of this Licence.

c. "Licensor" means the individual or entity that offers the Work under the terms of this Licence.

d. "Original Author" means the individual or entity who created the Work.

e. "Work" means the copyrightable work of authorship offered under the terms of this Licence.

f. "You" means an individual or entity exercising rights under this Licence who has not previously violated the terms of this Licence with respect to the Work, or who has received express permission from DEMOS to exercise rights under this Licence despite a previous violation.

2. Fair Use Rights.

Nothing in this licence is intended to reduce, limit, or restrict any rights arising from fair use, first sale or other limitations on the exclusive rights of the copyright owner under copyright law or other applicable laws.

3. Licence Grant.

Subject to the terms and conditions of this Licence, Licensor hereby grants You a worldwide, royalty-free, non-exclusive, perpetual (for the duration of the applicable copyright) licence to exercise the rights in the Work as stated below:

1. to reproduce the Work, to incorporate the Work into one or more Collective Works, and to reproduce the Work as incorporated in the Collective Works;

2. to distribute copies or phonorecords of, display publicly, perform publicly, and perform publicly by means of a digital audio transmission the Work including as incorporated in Collective Works;

The above rights may be exercised in all media and formats whether now known or hereafter devised. The above rights include the right to make such modifications as are technically necessary to exercise the rights in other media and formats. All rights not expressly granted by Licensor are hereby reserved.

4. Restrictions.

The licence granted in Section 3 above is expressly made subject to and limited by the following restrictions:

1. You may distribute, publicly display, publicly perform, or publicly digitally perform the Work only under the terms of this Licence, and You must include a copy of, or the Uniform Resource Identifier for, this Licence with every copy or phonorecord of the Work You distribute, publicly display, publicly perform, or publicly digitally perform. You may not offer or impose any terms on the Work that alter or restrict the terms of this Licence or the recipients' exercise of the rights granted hereunder. You may not sublicence the Work. You must keep intact all notices that refer to this Licence and to the disclaimer of warranties. You may not distribute, publicly display, publicly perform, or publicly digitally perform the Work with any technological measures that control access or use of the Work in a manner inconsistent with the terms of this Licence Agreement. The above applies to the Work as incorporated in a Collective Work, but this does not require the Collective Work apart from the Work itself to be made subject to the terms of this Licence. If You create a Collective Work, upon notice from any Licencor You must, to the extent practicable, remove from the Collective Work any reference to such Licensor or the Original Author, as requested.

2. You may not exercise any of the rights granted to You in Section 3 above in any manner that is primarily intended for or directed toward commercial advantage or private monetary compensation. The exchange of the Work for other copyrighted works by means of digital file-sharing or otherwise shall not be considered to be intended for or directed toward commercial advantage or private monetary compensation, provided there is no payment of any monetary compensation in connection with the exchange of copyrighted works.

3. If you distribute, publicly display, publicly perform, or publicly digitally perform the Work or any Collective Works, You must keep intact all copyright notices for the Work and give the Original Author credit reasonable to the medium or means You are utilizing by conveying the name (or pseudonym if applicable) of the Original Author if supplied; the title of the Work if supplied. Such credit may be implemented in any reasonable manner; provided, however, that in the case of a Collective Work, at a minimum such credit will appear where any other comparable authorship credit appears and in a manner at least as prominent as such other comparable authorship credit.

5. Representations, Warranties and Disclaimer

1. By offering the Work for public release under this Licence, Licensor represents and warrants that, to the best of Licensor's knowledge after reasonable inquiry:

1. Licensor has secured all rights in the Work necessary to grant the licence rights hereunder and to permit the lawful exercise of the rights granted hereunder without You having any obligation to pay any royalties, compulsory licence fees, residuals or any other payments;

2. The Work does not infringe the copyright, trademark, publicity rights, common law rights or any other right of any third party or constitute defamation, invasion of privacy or other tortious injury to any third party.

2. EXCEPT AS EXPRESSLY STATED IN THIS LICENCE OR OTHERWISE AGREED IN WRITING OR REQUIRED BY APPLICABLE LAW, THE WORK IS LICENCED ON AN "AS IS" BASIS, WITHOUT WARRANTIES OF ANY KIND, EITHER EXPRESS OR IMPLIED INCLUDING, WITHOUT LIMITATION, ANY WARRANTIES REGARDING THE CONTENTS OR ACCURACY OF THE WORK.

6. Limitation on Liability.

EXCEPT TO THE EXTENT REQUIRED BY APPLICABLE LAW, AND EXCEPT FOR DAMAGES ARISING FROM LIABILITY TO A THIRD PARTY RESULTING FROM BREACH OF THE WARRANTIES IN SECTION 5, IN NO EVENT WILL LICENSOR BE LIABLE TO YOU ON ANY LEGAL THEORY FOR ANY SPECIAL, INCIDENTAL, CONSEQUENTIAL, PUNITIVE OR EXEMPLARY DAMAGES ARISING OUT OF THIS LICENCE OR THE USE OF THE WORK, EVEN IF LICENSOR HAS BEEN ADVISED OF THE POSSIBILITY OF SUCH DAMAGES.

7. Termination

1. This Licence and the rights granted hereunder will terminate automatically upon any breach by You of the terms of this Licence. Individuals or entities who have received Collective Works from You under this Licence, however, will not have their licences terminated provided such individuals or entities remain in full compliance with those licences. Sections 1, 2, 5, 6, 7, and 8 will survive any termination of this Licence.

2. Subject to the above terms and conditions, the licence granted here is perpetual (for the duration of the applicable copyright in the Work). Notwithstanding the above, Licensor reserves the right to release the Work under different licence terms or to stop distributing the Work at any time; provided, however that any such election will not serve to withdraw this Licence (or any other licence that has been, or is required to be, granted under the terms of this Licence), and this Licence will continue in full force and effect unless terminated as stated above.

8. Miscellaneous

1. Each time You distribute or publicly digitally perform the Work or a Collective Work, DEMOS offers to the recipient a licence to the Work on the same terms and conditions as the licence granted to You under this Licence.

2. If any provision of this Licence is invalid or unenforceable under applicable law, it shall not affect the validity or enforceability of the remainder of the terms of this Licence, and without further action by the parties to this agreement, such provision shall be reformed to the minimum extent necessary to make such provision valid and enforceable.

3. No term or provision of this Licence shall be deemed waived and no breach consented to unless such waiver or consent shall be in writing and signed by the party to be charged with such waiver or consent.

4. This Licence constitutes the entire agreement between the parties with respect to the Work licensed here. There are no understandings, agreements or representations with respect to the Work not specified here. Licensor shall not be bound by any additional provisions that may appear in any communication from You. This Licence may not be modified without the mutual written agreement of DEMOS and You.